GUERNICA

GUERNICA

AND TOTAL WAR

IAN PATTERSON

Harvard University Press
Cambridge, Massachusetts
2007

Printed in the United States of America

First published in the United Kingdom by Profile Books Ltd,
58A Hatton Garden, London EC IN 8LX

Library of Congress Cataloging-in-Publication Data

Patterson, Ian.
Guernica and total war / Ian Patterson.
p. cm.
Includes bibliographical references.
ISBN-13: 978-0-674-02484-7 (alk. paper)
ISBN-10: 0-674-02484-2 (alk. paper)
1. Guernica (Spain)—History—Bombardment, 1937.
2. Spain—History—Civil War, 1936-1939—Atrocities.
3. Bombing, Aerial—Moral and ethical aspects.
4. Combatants and noncombatants (International law)
5. War—Moral and ethical aspects.
I. Title.
DP269.27.G8P27 2007
946.081 48—dc22   2006101588

CONTENTS

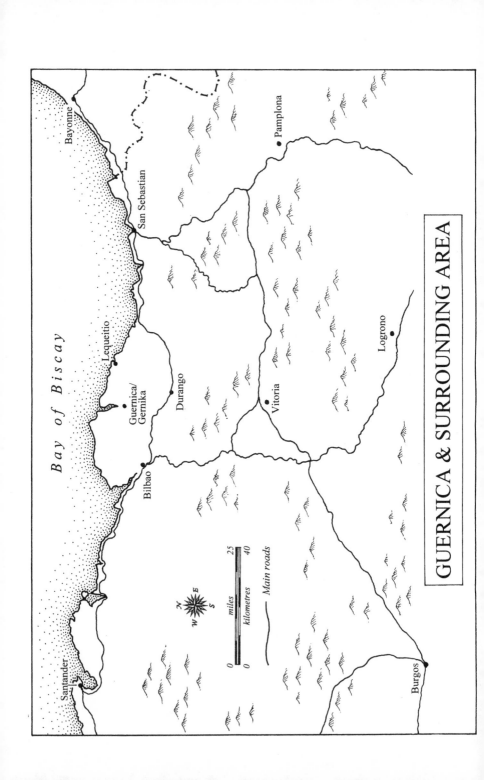

GUERNICA & SURROUNDING AREA

To my father

INTRODUCTION

I believe that memory and imagination, not nuclear weapons,
are the great deterrents.

Martha Gellhorn

In Fernando Arrabal's play *Guernica*, one of the characters is
simply called the Writer. Bombs are intermittently falling as
he self-importantly communicates his ideas to another character, the Journalist. 'This heroic and paradoxical people,
which reflects the spirit of Lorca's poems, Goya's paintings,
and Buñuel's films, is demonstrating, in this dreadful war,
its courage, its capacity for suffering, its … [*His voice fades
away*].' Later he is heard again, still on the same theme: 'What
a complex and heart-rending people! Put that down – no,
say that the complexity of this heart-rending people flour-
ishes in a spontaneous fashion in this cruel and fratricidal
war. [*Pleased with himself*] Not bad, eh? [*He hesitates.*] No, no,
leave out that sentence. ' And so on. His refrain, heard from
time to time, is 'What a novel I shall make out of all this.
What a novel! Or a play, perhaps, and even a film. And what
a film!'

Absurd, self-mocking and comic though this is, it high-
lights one of the focal problems of the modern world. How
can our powers of thought – of language, or of art – cope with

the enormities of war, in particular with the terrifying force of aerial bombardment. How can they express the range of inexpressible terror and grief and fear without becoming pompous or exaggerated or sentimental or – like many of the films and documentaries that have followed the disaster of 9/11 – simply inadequate to the scale and meaning of the event?

One of the most fearsome ideas to emerge in the course of the twentieth century was the idea of total war – the belief that the most effective way of winning wars was by the obliteration, or the threat of obliteration, of the civilian population of the enemy's towns and cities by means of an annihilating attack from the air. The first, and still in some ways the most striking, demonstration that this could be done came in April 1937, when the ancient Basque town of Guernica was almost completely destroyed by the blast and incendiary bombs of the German Condor Legion. Since then, civilians have more and more frequently been made the target of wartime bombing, as death, destruction and demoralisation have grown increasingly intertwined in the search for rapid victory. The US military's strategy of 'shock and awe' in its attack on Baghdad in the spring of 2003 suggests that the same approach is still around in the twenty-first century.

Picasso's painting in response to the bombing made Guernica the most famous image of total war, and articulated the terror of it so potently that the picture has become almost synonymous with a sense of outrage and condemnation. Merely possessing a reproduction of it in Spain during the Franco era was an imprisonable offence. But it was only one of a huge number of cultural artefacts – paintings, films, novels, poems, plays – to explore the idea of indiscriminate death from the air, and the new ways in which this makes us think about death, both our own and other people's.

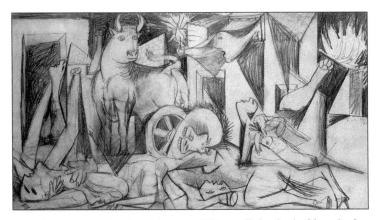

1. Composition Study *9 May 1937. This small sketch, the fifteenth of Picasso's preliminary sketches for his painting, was the one which first mapped out its compositional relations, two days before he started work on the painting itself, which was 250 times larger.*

From the beginning of the twentieth century there was a startling growth in novelistic fantasies of worldwide disaster, often fuelled by fears of science, or other races, or the working class, or invasion. Starting from Guernica, this book sets out to trace one of the forms taken by these fears: the idea of being bombed – the modern version of the sky falling on one's head. Picasso's painting owes part of its cultural success to the fact that it represents the tip of a vast iceberg that has been an intrinsic part of the cultural thought of the West for most of the last hundred years.

This is not a work of military history, though it draws gratefully on the work of many military historians. It's a book about how modern men and women have responded to living with a new kind of power and a new focus of fear. Fear of death is hard-wired into all of us, and always has been, but the way we imagine death changes, and therefore death's role and presence in our culture changes too. Fear of death has its counterpart in aggression, too, so our capacities for imagining and enacting aggression equally shape, and are shaped by, this new and developing culture.

The evocation of the indescribable, the sublime of beauty or of terror, calls on powers that properly lie within the realm of the aesthetic. But all elements of culture at least reference such things, often using the same vocabulary in an attempt to communicate the scope of the emotion or state of mind they create. In 1938 Bertrand Russell quoted Giacomo Leopardi's poetic description of a volcanic eruption, and the desolation it causes, in order to summon up this state of mind:

> here were famous towns,
> Which the implacable mountain, thundering forth
> Molten streams from its fiery mouth, destroyed
> With all their habitants. Now all around
> Lies crushed 'neath one vast ruin.

He then drily commented that 'these results can now be achieved by men. They have been achieved at Guernica; perhaps before long they will be achieved where as yet London stands ... There is no hope for the world unless power can be tamed ... for science has made it inevitable that all must live or all must die.'

How have people responded to the power of aerial bombardment, as it was revealed in the bombing of Guernica? And what (if anything) has the world learned in the years since then about taming or controlling it?

THE FOLDED LIE

The decade before the Second World War was a period of

intensifying conflicts. Economic and social crisis intensified across the world throughout the ten years from 1929. But of all the crises that occurred, the Spanish Civil War, which lasted from July 1936 to March 1939, was the one that most vividly embodied the political, ethical or religious hopes and fears of people in Europe and America. Some saw it as a rehearsal for the next war, some as the last-ditch stand of Christian civilisation, some as the battle of social progress against the entrenched interests of reaction and fascism. It was an opportunity for a few capitalists to make or lose money, for some politicians to make propaganda, and for many writers and artists to show in starker terms the divisions simmering or already at work in their own societies. It attracted commentators from all parts of the political spectrum, many of them with axes to grind and a willingness to spread rumour and untruth in their writings.

Looking back in September 1939 from the relative security of the USA, W. H. Auden called the 1930s a 'low dishonest decade', and so, at certain levels, it was. It was convenient for commentators during the Cold War years to claim that Auden was referring only to deluded left-wing or utopian political attitudes, but his intended criticism was wider than that. Everywhere, governments, politicians, demagogues, radio stations, military leaders, newspapers, writers and film-makers were busily shaping and reshaping visions of reality to suit their own interests or their own points of view. As the historian Piers Brendon has put it, 'All the major occurrences of the day were the subject of organised deception which ranged from the big, amplified lie to a delicate economy with the truth ... The Depression years witnessed the dissemination of falsehood on a hitherto unprecedented scale ... Political power obscured knowledge and economic catastrophe darkened understanding.' Small wonder that more people than ever were confused, uncertain, looking for answers, or trying to find information they could trust. Demand for such information grew as old habits of deference and trust, undermined by the First World War, were replaced by new and different ideals. The 'old gang' no longer had authority, and nobody quite knew who the 'new gang' were – or rather there was no agreement about it. One consequence was that all levels of society and all means of communication were affected by battles over the perception and representation of events, while simultaneously being shaped by the enormous developments in communication which fuelled and intensified the propaganda struggle. Questions of truth and reality coloured social, political and economic movements all over the globe.

For many in Britain, America and elsewhere – those with secure jobs and a steady or growing level of prosperity – these questions were not urgent. The social movements of the early 1930s tended to involve mainly idealists or those with an already developed social conscience. But even those who were not troubled by the spectacle of hunger, unemployment or the rise of fascism found their dreams shaped by the novels and magazine stories they read, and by what they heard on the radio or saw on the screen of their local cinema. Their psyches, whether they knew it or not, were absorbing anxieties which others were articulating and which would increasingly shape their own outlook as the decade wore on.

This was more consciously true for the more consciously intellectual artistry of poets, painters and serious novelists, who either felt a need to address contemporary issues in their work or found that their thinking about the world demanded new kinds of expression. Many of the avant-garde artists in the years following the First World War were looking for ways of modifying or reforming their stylistic approach, partly as they assimilated the impact of the war. In some countries they were driven into exile by hostile regimes; others turned against their own unsympathetic cultures in favour of the new justice promised by the USSR. The French surrealist movement broke up in acrimonious arguments about political commitment, while at the same time beginning to capture the imagination of a public whose disturbed dreams were looking for some visible counterpart in the world. New logics, new landscapes and new public voices characterised artistic production. The adjective itself, 'new', was in demand, as in anthologies of 'new writing' like *New Signatures* and *New Country*, or magazines like *New Verse*, in England, and *New Masses* and *New Directions* in the USA. New inventions promised heaven or threatened hell. At the same time, the need for novelty changed the perception of time, made it almost tangible, brought change and the future closer, and threatened, in a variety of ways, an end to the present. It was widely agreed, in many different areas of life, that things could not go on as they were, even if people wanted them to – which many didn't. If spring was here, could autumn be far behind?

Nostalgia for an old England that was disappearing in an industrial society bled over into a proleptic nostalgia for what would have to be given up in the name of a better civilisation. Newspapers, weekly periodicals, a flood of books, cinema newsreels, radio, and conversation in buses, workplaces, shops and pubs retailed information about the changing political face of Europe, especially in Germany

after 1933. It was a world well evoked in Louis MacNeice's
Autumn Journal – a world of

> Conferences, adjournments, ultimatums,
>   Flights in the air, castles in the air,
> The autopsy of treaties, dynamite under the bridges,
>   The end of *laissez faire*.

The Soviet Union's supporters in the Communist parties
of non-Communist countries were exacerbating already
existing inner social tensions in the name of the struggle yet
to come. Across the world, Japan saw itself as the imperial
saviour of Asia, and invaded and occupied Manchuria in
1931 to create a wall of defence against Soviet Communism.
At one extreme, totalitarian governments were being
installed across Europe, while, at the other, people all over
the western world laughed at Mickey Mouse cartoons. Non-
aggression pacts signalled the postponement of aggression
rather than the triumph of peace – something which the
League of Nations in Geneva seemed decreasingly capable
of delivering, especially after it failed to halt Mussolini's
invasion of Abyssinia (Ethiopia) in 1935, or breaches in the
non-intervention pact during the Spanish Civil War.

When the civil war broke out, in July 1936, Spain scarcely
figured in most people's awareness of European events. It
tended to be thought of as changeable, hot, self-absorbed,
primitive, feudal, Catholic, 'sunny' – the first newsreel to
report the civil war was titled 'Death in Sunny Spain' – and
generally marginal to the modern world, even allowing for
the limited amount of modernisation which had been introduced by Primo de Rivera's dictatorship during the 1920s.

Spain had remained neutral during the First World War

(although Basque seamen had risked attack from U-boats to continue exports of iron ore to Britain), and generally seemed to be outside the main currents of European politics. The Republican government of Manuel Azaña which came peacefully to power in 1931 made fewer changes than his supporters hoped for, but made plenty of political enemies in the process. Azaña attempted to weaken the Catholic Church's hold on the state by secularising education and allowing civil marriage, and he instituted a degree of land reform. He also introduced tax increases for the rich, and reorganised the cripplingly expensive but outdated and ill-equipped army.

Unrest increased, Azaña's government was replaced by a centre–right coalition in late 1933, and a left-wing uprising in the following year was rapidly put down by armed force. Rape, torture and death – the brutal methods of control used by the troops in Spain's rebellious Moroccan colony – were consciously used as methods of reprisal and repression by the de facto commander of army operations in Asturias, General Francisco Franco. The historian Burnett Bolloten quotes a description of those times, written by a conservative Republican: 'The accused were tortured in the jails; prisoners were executed without trial in the courtyards of the barracks, and eyes were closed to the persecutions and atrocities committed by the police in those sixteen months.' In a 1935 report on the repression, which she had investigated at first hand, the former British MP Leah Manning described a clandestine encounter with an eyewitness. '"No one will believe these stories, Margarita," I said despairingly. "I shall be unable to convince anyone in England that such things can happen in a civilised country unless I can take back documentary evidence."' Manning's book was more than usually careful in its search for accurate testimony, but, for all her faith in documentary evidence, it had little effect on British public opinion, let alone government policy. It suited the British authorities to have a strong anti-socialist government in Spain. They preferred not to know too much about the upheavals of what the Spanish Left later called *el bienio negro*, the two black years.

But in reaction to the violence and repression, and despite exaggerated and scaremongering claims by the Right, the next election in Spain, February 1936, saw a victory for the Left, in the form of the loose coalition of socialist and Republican forces that constituted the Popular Front. This created anxiety for the British and American governments, and for investors, but failed to bring an end to the demonstrations, strikes, political murders, attacks on churches, occupations and other manifestations of growing extremism. In fact these got worse. Regional loyalties found yet more dramatic expression, and the country became more divided as regional, sectarian, political and religious allegiances became increasingly polarised.

On 17 July 1936, nine months before the destruction of Guernica, General Franco launched a right-wing military rebellion against the Republican government of Spain. The Nationalists had no very clear programme behind their rebellion, beyond a desire to institute an authoritarian government that would centralise power and put an end to the recent reforms. Within this general aim, there were a variety of different attitudes – including support for the monarchy, for a dictatorship, for the Catholic Church, for the old order in general, and implacable hostility to socialism, freemasonry, communism, Jews, anarchism, Basque independence and social reform. The government was supported by an even less homogeneous alliance of liberals, socialists, communists, anarcho-syndicalists, modernisers, trade unionists, intellectuals, artists and writers. Three out of the four Basque provinces, otherwise not deeply involved in these struggles, supported the Republican government, which was committed to giving them increased independence. The rebels had been confident that there would be little resistance, and that this would be quickly overcome and a new national government be installed in Madrid. But the principal cities failed to rally to the uprising, and armed workers set about organising against it under the banners of whichever left-wing organisations were dominant locally. Spain was split between the rural areas in the north and west, which supported the insurgents (along with an enclave between Seville and Cadiz in the south), and central and southern Spain, including Madrid, which continued loyal to the elected government. A prolonged civil war seemed inevitable, and Franco requested military support from Germany and Italy, who responded with large amounts of men and *matériel*. German aid was particularly focused on the air, in the form of what became the six-thousand-strong Condor Legion, a substantial array of fighter squadrons, bombers and reconnaissance and other aeroplanes with which the German High Command was able to try out new techniques and develop new strategies which it was able to put into practice when the Second World War broke out. Italy sent large numbers of bombers, fighters, personnel and weaponry. Russia sent aid to the Republican government, mostly in the form of tanks and planes, and an International Brigade of politically conscious volunteers from all over the world provided a core of fighters, some of them experienced, who were useful for propaganda purposes.

Despite the widely recognised intervention of Franco's

allies – there were fifty thousand Italian troops in Spain and about ten thousand Germans, including the six thousand of the Condor Legion – Britain and France quickly declared their intention not to intervene on either side in Spain, and a London-based 'Non-Intervention Committee', involving twenty-seven countries, was set up. It was part of the Baldwin government's policy of appeasement to do everything it could to discourage 'Bolshevism'. As the Germans and Italians paid no attention to the undertakings of the Committee, its chief result was effectively to provide support to Franco by imposing an economic embargo and political isolation on the elected government of Spain. The war was protracted and bloody, and lasted until the surrender of Madrid and the final defeat of the Republic at the end of March 1939.

When the war broke out, the Americans who were attending the Anti-Fascist Olympic Games in Barcelona (convened as a protest against the 1936 Berlin Olympics) were evacuated from Barcelona by order of the Catalan government. They went, with Spanish refugees and with men and women of many other nationalities, by boat to France. The American poet Muriel Rukeyser was among them, and in *Mediterranean* (1938) she evokes a moving sense not only of the sadness of exile, but also of the hypocrisy surrounding the war:

> We see Europe break like stone,
> hypocrite sovereignties go down
> before this war the age must win.

Accusations of hypocrisy were directed at most governments' response to the war, in America, in France and in Britain. In November 1936, four months after the outbreak of the civil war, the Holborn and West Central London Committee for Spanish Medical Aid published a pamphlet called *Spain and Us* which typifies this thinking. One thread above all united the distinguished contributors, which was their 'bewilderment' at the press treatment of the insurgents, who were being presented as 'a band of noble patriots', while the legitimate government of the country was described as if it was a 'gang of murderous ruffians'. All the short articles were rational, well-balanced pieces, lamenting the 'humbugging' nature of the British government, the misrepresentation and the lies, and the whole factitious policy of non-intervention that accompanied the official British attitude to the war.

Given that governments always lie, especially about foreign-policy issues and war, it might seem surprising that so many people felt so strongly about it at this particular moment, in 1936. But it was a moment in which an unusually large number of different strands of anxiety, expectation, hope, fear, apprehension and uncertainty were crystallising around whatever offered the right sort of hold. The Spanish Civil War did this, as Louis MacNeice elegantly explained in *Autumn Journal* three years later.

next day [we] took the boat
    For home, forgetting Spain, not realising
That Spain would soon denote
    Our grief, our aspirations;
Not knowing that our blunt
    Ideals would find their whetstone, that our spirit
Would find its frontier on the Spanish front,
    Its body in a rag-tag army.

And when news came of the bombing of Guernica – by

2. Like many paintings in the European tradition, the images from the Spanish Civil War often use religious or biblical themes in a secular context. This woodcut, by Gwen Raverat, produced in support of Cambridge Medical Aid for Spain in 1937, despite its bombing planes, has powerful echoes of the theme of the Flight into Egypt.

German planes, with German bombs – the anger at the political hypocrisy which pretended that the war was exclusively a Spanish affair fused with many other fears to create an international wave of outrage which elevated the event to symbolic status. The novelist Heinrich Mann spoke for the anti-Nazi population of Germany at home and in exile when he said that 'the flames of Guernica also light up Germany. If only the world could see it! Freedom for Germany is at the same time freedom for the whole world from the abominable threat of "total war", from the bewitchment of peoples through mendacious "ideologies", and from atrocities like Guernica.'

In a complicated way, as Mann's words demonstrate, Guernica was also a propaganda gift. In situations or conflicts like this, people are always looking for some piece of incontrovertible evidence of the guilt, or the irredeemable criminality, of the other side. The tragedy of Guernica provided that. It showed, adaptably and in a way that nothing else so clearly could, the complete inhumanity of the enemy, whether in the form of the Spanish Nationalists, Nazi Germany, Mussolini's Fascism, totalitarianism, modern warfare, technology, or simply the forces opposed to social progress. That was why the bombing was denied. And that is why the Nationalists in Spain and their sympathisers around the world – also aiming to demonstrate the inhumanity of their enemy – set about spreading the tale that Guernica had been blown up by Asturian miners.

This disinformation was a tactic that had enough success to complicate the issue for years. One of the questions to be investigated in the chapters that follow is how it came about that such an unequivocal happening as the destruction of a town by aerial bombardment carried such a profound ideological valency that people actually wanted to believe that it never happened. Especially as what then seemed to be a unique, unprecedented event, the intentional bombing of defenceless European civilians, was soon to be the fate of huge numbers of quite ordinary people in their quite ordinary homes all over Europe.

1

'GUERNIKA'S THERMITE RAIN'

Euskadi's mines supply the ore
To feed the Nazi dogs of war:
Guernika's thermite rain transpires
In doom on Oxford's dreaming spires:
In Hitler's frantic mental haze
Already Hull and Cardiff blaze,
And Paul's grey dome rocks to the blast
Of air-torpedoes screaming past.

Edgell Rickword, 'To the Wife of Any Non-Interventionist
Statesman' (*Left Review*, March 1938)

A SYMBOLIC EVENT

Guernica (or Gernika in the Basque spelling that was
adopted in the late nineteenth century), a small Basque
Catholic town, lying high up among protecting hills in the
province of Vizcaya in the area of northern Spain that the
Basques call Euskadi, became world famous on 27 April
1937, in the tenth month of the Spanish Civil War, after it had
been almost completely destroyed by bombs. In the space
of a few hours, during the previous afternoon and evening,
this thriving and peaceful historic market town was largely
reduced to rubble, its inhabitants killed, injured or driven

into exile from their homes. It was the first time that a completely unmilitarised, undefended, ordinary civilian town in Europe had been subjected to this sort of devastating attack from the air. Yet it was not simply the scale of the destruction that made it a cause célèbre, unparalleled though that was. What kept Guernica at the centre of international attention for so long, and imbued it with the symbolic resonance it still retains today, was a series of crucial additional factors which made it a case study in propaganda, ethics and international law.

The first, and in some ways the most important, of these was the categorical denial of responsibility by General Franco's rebel forces. The statement broadcast on Radio Requeté, as quoted by the historian Herbert H. Southworth, read, 'The news published by the ridiculous president of the republic of Euskadi concerning the fires provoked by the bombs of our airplanes at Guernica is completely false. Our aviators have received no orders to bomb this town … Unable to hold back our troops, the Reds have destroyed everything.' In a series of extraordinary and contradictory statements, the insurgents claimed first of all that there had been no bombing of Guernica, then that it had been only slightly bombed, and finally that it had been blown up and burned from within by Basque Republicans and Catalonian anarchists in an attempt to implicate the Nationalist forces in an atrocity. As one eyewitness, a Catholic priest, put it, 'This calumny seemed to me almost worse than the burning of the town: to murder poor innocent people and then to attribute to them the most horrible crime of this war.' The second reason was that Guernica was the symbolic capital of the Basques, seat of their ceremonial government and home of their ancient and fiercely defended democratic freedoms.

3. *In the BBC magazine* The Listener *for the week ending 5 May 1937 there appeared two photographs: one, of the ruins of Guernica, was juxtaposed with this image of the peaceful town, taken in the days before the civil war.*

And the third reason for Guernica's elevation to historic status was the huge commemorative panel, eleven feet tall by twenty-five feet long, painted in black, grey and white by Picasso for the Spanish pavilion at the Paris World's Fair in 1937, which soon became an instantly recognisable depiction of the victims of modern war. The painting was finished on 6 June, and was installed in the just-completed pavilion some two weeks later.

The story of how the painting came to be made, its elevation to iconic status, and its long subsequent odyssey and eventual exhibition in Spain (though not, as yet, in the Basque country) has been well told in at least two recent books (by Gijs van Hensbergen and by Russell Martin), and I shall have little to say about it here. But, appropriately enough, Picasso's painting has been dogged by a history of

controversy that echoes and parallels the controversies surrounding the destruction of the town of Guernica itself. That
event was translated over the next forty years into so many
different ideological terms by its observers, by propagandists,
by historians, by the moral and political debates it fuelled,
and by the fate of its witnesses, that the original question
of responsibility became almost completely obscured. The
bombing was variously presented in terms of martyrdom,
sacrifice, heroism, necessity, barbarism, cruelty, scientific
warfare and melodrama; as a warning about the nature of
modern warfare, even as a glimpse of an inevitable future.
All these depictions were accurate in one way or another,
though not all were truthful. In that respect, as in many
others, the earliest reports are the best and the most reliable
– especially those of the *Times* special correspondent George
L. Steer, author of the definitive account of the Basque war,
The Tree of Gernika (1938). One additional reason gave the
bombing of Guernica additional poignancy. Terrible events
like wars or natural disasters always set the lives of the ordinary people caught up in them against a starkly contrast-
ing background of the vast impersonality of natural or social
forces. The sheer domesticity of this small market town, in
the middle of a civil war it had not sought, pulverised for
purely contingent and tactical reasons, captured the sympathetic imagination of millions of powerless onlookers.

News of both the bombing and the Francoist denials of it
were flashed round the world almost simultaneously, initi-
ating a bitter contest for the true facts which continued for
years. Had it not been for the presence in Bilbao of some
remarkable foreign correspondents, working for the Reuters
news agency and for one Belgian and several British newspapers, the real nature of the events of 26 April might not

have been known until decades later. Certainly the bombing of Guernica would never have taken on its symbolic significance. So deeply was the event embedded in the conflict-ridden memories of the citizens of post-civil-war Spain that it took forty years for the truth to be unequivocally established. Even now remnants of the old lies still occasionally resurface in books and newspapers, and people in Spain are still reluctant to speak out about the things they know or the things they saw, old men and women still afraid, even now, of punishment or reprisals if they do. This was a *civil war*, after all (although it was not until the 1960s that the Franco regime began to allow explicit mention of this), with both sides struggling for military and civil power in Spain, and for authority in the world. And this authority included the credibility of their military and political announcements.

The collection of enough detailed information and impartial eyewitness accounts to clarify the turbid waters of Franco's Spain and establish an unequivocal narrative of the events of 26 April 1937 therefore took far longer than normal. Under Franco, all writing – and especially historical accounts of the civil war and its aftermath – was subject to heavy censorship, backed up by a feared and powerful state police. Only with Franco's death in 1975 and Spain's return to democracy did it become possible to start gathering those accounts within the country and publishing them, and by then of course many of the participants were dead, missing or far away. Despite this, a great deal of important work was done. Chief among the historians of the event remains the American journalist and historian Herbert Southworth, who had already spent much of his life persistently tracing and documenting everything written about the bombing of Guernica in order to disprove the Nationalist version of events and to show beyond all doubt that the destruction was the work of the German Condor Legion. The work of the oral historians who collected and printed local residents' accounts of the bombing provides further valuable and incontrovertible evidence. Nobody now, however self-deluding, can still believe that the Republicans burned Guernica. That we possess such minute detail about the operation and its subsequent reporting is thanks to the tenacity of people like Southworth who wanted to remove the smokescreen of religious, political and ideological mendacity and self-interest from the historical record.

Recognising the crucial role played by the press in the controversy, Southworth divided the foundational articles into three categories. First, the initial bulletins sent out by foreign correspondents and local stringers, based on their own observations, on statements by Basque leaders, and on follow-up stories 'such as interviews with captured German pilots or with refugees from Guernica, written in Bilbao, at the frontier, or in France'. Second, the 'reports, communiqués, and declarations published in the Spanish Nationalist press as an immediate reaction to news of the bombing in the foreign press and to statements of Basque officials in Bilbao'. And, third, the accounts of foreign journalists who visited Guernica after it had been taken by the Nationalists on 29 April, 'forwarded between that date and 6 May'. In all essentials, the materials produced during these three stages provided the basis for the whole of the subsequent controversy.

The *Daily Express* correspondent in Spain, Noel Monks, an Australian, had just been expelled from the Nationalist south of Spain. He had arrived in the Basque country to cover the story of 'Potato Jones', captain of one of three

British merchant ships (each commanded by a Captain
Jones, the captains thus being known by nicknames derived
from their cargo) attempting to run food into Bilbao, against
Admiralty instructions. After that, on Sunday 25 April, he
visited Durango, 'or what was left of it'. This small town a
few miles to the south of Guernica had been systematically
bombed by German and Italian planes almost four weeks
earlier. It was not, as Steer says, 'the most terrible bombardment of a civil population in the history of the world up to
March 31st 1937', but it was certainly the worst that Europe
had experienced. A hundred and twenty-seven civilians,
including thirteen nuns and two priests, had been killed,
and 121 more died later of their injuries.

Having inspected the ruins of the town and its churches,
Monks was then taken by his driver to lunch with a family in
Guernica. He described that introduction to Guernica eight-
een years later in his autobiographical memoir *Eye Witness*.

There were two old parents, a grown son and a daughter.
A younger son was away at the front. We didn't talk much
about the war ... The old man was worried. Someone had
told him that the Pope had excommunicated all Basque
Catholics for not throwing in their lot with Franco. To a
man who had been a devout Catholic all his life and who
had reared a Catholic family, that was a matter of grave
anxiety. But his worries were over when I saw him next
evening. He was lying a few feet from where his home
had been, a mangled, tangled mass of flesh. One hand
was clutching what seemed to be a bundle of rags. His
wife had been inside those rags when the bombs began
falling. Pieces of her were strewn over the cobblestones.

but most had no reason to leave and nowhere to go except to swell the number of refugees in Bilbao, within its defensive 'iron ring' of fortifications.

It was Monday, market day. Because of the blockade of the ports, and the impossibility of getting stuff through the enemy front line, which had been coming relentlessly closer during the preceding weeks, food was already becoming so scarce that there was a burgeoning black market. A kilo of coffee could cost as much as a quarter of a labourer's annual income. The traditional livestock market had officially been discontinued because of the war, but, although the authorities in Bilbao had called for the abandonment of all markets during the hostilities, there was no other way for local farmers and producers to sell their food, or for the townspeople and the people who lived in the surrounding countryside to get hold of it. So the market continued. Ronald Fraser, in his oral history of the civil war, *Blood of Spain* (1979), quotes a local priest, Father José Axunguiz, as warning his parishioners not to go to the Guernica market that day: 'It was an outing for the youth; buses brought people from as far away as Lequeitio on the coast. The people lacked war training ... Those of us who lived virtually on the front, as at Larquina, had learnt the importance of building good shelters. But in Guernica they hadn't taken adequate precautions; the shelters were rudimentary.' This was not entirely just, but it shows the extent to which people were already afraid. Many of the shelters may have been rudimentary, but there were some solid ones too. They had been constructed on the orders of the mayor, José de Labauria, after the bombing of Durango, and there were five in or near the centre of the town. They were made with stout pine stakes placed vertically, with more of the same laid horizontally on top, above which were two layers of sandbags, then steel sheets, then two more layers of sandbags. Steer describes others – cellars covered with sandbags, with a similarly protected entrance: 'a cardboard at the door painted ornamentally *refugio* showed where the people had to dive'.

Thomas and Morgan-Witts, in their not entirely reliable reconstruction of that day, say that half the market stalls were empty (partly because of a lack of goods to sell and a lack of the money to buy them) and that some farmers packed up and left early. But it seems likely that, even with a reduced market, the figure of somewhere between seven and ten thousand people remaining in the town, including the refugees, is an accurate one. As he describes it in his book, Steer makes the market sound almost idyllic, somewhat romantically evoking a timeless pastoral scene, with solid-wheeled farm carts rolling towards the town, pulled by oxen. 'Basque peasants in their long puckered market smocks walked backwards in front of them, mesmerising the oxen to Gernika with their slim wands ... Others were driving sheep to market.' Suddenly, at 4.30, the single church bell started to ring out the air-raid warning and the scene changed completely as people ran for cover.

A single aeroplane appeared, identified by Steer as a Heinkel He-111, thought by some others to have been a Dornier Do-17E, and in either case possibly piloted by the Condor Legion's most experienced and accomplished flier, Major Rudolf von Moreau of the VB/88 experimental squadron based at Burgos with the K/88 bomber squadron. Whatever it was, and whoever was flying it, it flew menacingly low over the town, and dropped six (or in some accounts twelve) bombs and, some sources suggest, a shower of incendiaries. They fell together, on and around the crowded railway station. Thomas and Morgan-Witts quote Juan Silliaco, a volunteer fireman, describing their effects on a group of women and children, in words that have often been quoted since. 'They were lifted high into the air, maybe twenty feet or so, and they started to break up. Legs, arms, heads, and bits and pieces flying everywhere.' Aguirreamalloa disputes the authenticity of this, claiming that no such person as Juan Silliaco existed; but, whether or not that is true, a similarly vivid image also appears in other accounts. The fragmentation of human beings stays in the imagination. Bombs from a second Heinkel shortly afterwards cut the phone line to Bilbao, and the pilot machine-gunned the town at random before leaving. There may have been other planes. Fifteen or twenty minutes passed during which nothing else happened.

People began to think the attack was over. They came out of the *refugios* to inspect the damage and to help the injured and fight the fires. The parish priest, Father Aronategui, was walking towards the railway station with sacraments for the dying. Then a new wave of bombers approached – more He-111s, followed by Heinkel He-51 fighter-bombers and Messerschmitt fighters from J-88 (Jagdgruppe-88, or 88-Hunters – in the Nazis' schoolboy code, '88' stood for 'HH' (H being the eighth letter of the alphabet), or 'Heil Hitler'). Near the bridge they bombed a sweet factory, which went up in fierce flames, fed by the sugar. Soon a thick cloud of smoke and dust hung over the town, choking those who tried to go back down into the cellars and *refugios* and obscuring the bombers' view and encouraging them – if they needed encouragement – to drop their bombs indiscriminately on the buildings beneath. This they did.

Unable to take adequate shelter in the town, and harried

in the less smoky areas by low-flying fighters, which were shooting up anything that moved, great numbers of people started to run into the fields around the town, sheltering under trees where they could. The He-51s and the Messerschmitt fighters dived low over them, dropping grenades and machine-gunning everyone indiscriminately – old and young, men, women, babies, nuns and livestock.

After five o'clock, about a quarter past, people started to hear the low, heavy buzz of larger bombers, this time the much heavier Junkers Ju-52s – trimotor planes, converted to bombing from transport use. The historian Hugh Thomas calls them 'the old spectre of the Spanish War'. They were approaching up the valley from the south-west, and with them came more of the new He-111s. These were probably accompanied by some Italian planes, Savoia S-81s, from the squadron based south-east of Burgos at Soria, although not all authorities are agreed on this. The planes bombed the town continuously, in waves about twenty minutes apart, for over two more hours, until about 7.30. The Heinkel He-51s – relatively slow planes used for strafing and low-level bombing – could carry up to six 10-kg anti-personnel fragmentation bombs, and had open cockpits, so the pilots could chuck grenades out over the side. These were based nearby at Vitoria, and could return to refuel and reload before setting off again to keep up the carpet-bombing momentum. The three squadrons from the airfield at Burgos also had time to refuel and return for another bombing run. There seem to have been at least twenty-three of the Ju-52s, dropping a combination of high-explosive bombs, of various sizes up to 250-kg, 10-kg anti-personnel bombs, and thermite incendiaries, full of white phosphorus, which burned at temperatures up to 2,500°C. The fighters, which in other circumstances

4. As Guernica burned, the flames caused by incendiary bombs lit up the sky for fifteen miles around.

would have been escorting the bombers and defending them against a Republican attack, had nothing to do except strafe the people who were trying to escape. And the panicking or burning livestock. The German historian Klaus Maier has calculated that in all about 35 tonnes of explosive was dropped.

The bombs reduced much of the town to rubble, and the incendiaries set fires which spread quickly and grew in intensity until the whole town was burning, causing the pink glow that Steer saw from fifteen miles away. A French journalist who visited the town five days later found fires still smouldering or burning 'under the stones or tiles'. Nobody can say with certainty exactly how many died and how many were injured during the three or three and a half hours of the attack. The figures most often quoted are 1,654 dead and 889 injured. Recent researchers have suggested a much lower figure, of between 200 and 300, but there seems no reason to disbelieve Noel Monks' report in the *Daily Express* for 1 May, in which he described counting 600 corpses, while many more were being dug out of the ruins. In an earlier report he hauntingly described the fields as 'strewn with hundreds of dead sheep', machine-gunned by the Germans.

EYEWITNESS ACCOUNTS

The first official news of Guernica's bombing was broadcast on Radio Bilbao between ten and twelve in the morning of 27 April 1937. At noon, a statement by President Aguirre was broadcast; it also appeared in the Basque press that morning. 'The German airmen in the service of the Spanish rebels have bombarded Gernika, burning the historic town which is held in such veneration by all Basques. They have sought to wound us in the most sensitive of our patriotic sentiments, once more making it entirely clear what Euskadi may expect of those who do not hesitate to destroy us down to the very sanctuary that records the centuries of our liberty and democracy.' In the earliest reports, German involvement and responsibility were clear.

In addition to the carpet-bombing of an undefended civilian area, the other new element in the bombing of this historic Basque town was the fact that the high explosive was followed by thousands of thermite bombs. These created such intense fires among the old wood-framed buildings which made up most of the town that the place became an inferno. Both the town and its inhabitants seemed to have been removed from the world. To many people it demonstrated on a small scale, and with appropriately inhuman ruthlessness, what might happen to even – or especially – the great cities of Europe in the event of another major war. And of course it suited the German High Command for others to believe that it possessed the capability to wreak such havoc. Steer's first account, published in *The Times*, and accompanied by a powerful editorial, was the first and most influential description of the bombing. It has been reproduced often enough, but it still deserves a few extracts here. It appeared under the capitalised headline 'The Tragedy of Guernica', and called the raid an event 'unparalleled in military history'. Steer makes it abundantly clear that there had been no military objective. 'A factory producing armaments lay outside the town and was untouched. So were two barracks some distance from the town.' The measured but nonetheless outraged tone of the piece continues with the conclusion that 'The object of the bombardment was seemingly the demoralisation of the civil population and the destruction of the cradle of the Basque race.' Most shocking is Steer's insistence on the entirely calculated nature of the raid. He describes the tactics of the bombers, including the slaughter of the sheep, adding ironically that 'they may be of interest to students of the new military science'. And right from the start he makes it completely clear that it was incendiary bombs which were responsible for most of the destruction. Upwards of three thousand of the gleaming aluminium tubes, weighing two pounds each and packed with silver powder, were unleashed. 'The only counter-measures the Basques could employ,' Steer wrote towards the end of the report, 'for they do not possess sufficient airplanes to face the insurgent fleet, were those provided by the heroism of the Basque clergy. These blessed and prayed for the kneeling crowds – Socialists, Anarchists, and Communists, as well as the declared faithful – in the crumbling dugouts.'

Many of the key features of the phenomenon of Guernica

are referenced in his article: the sense of the event as a 'tragedy'; the importance of the town in Basque culture; the 'powerful fleet' of bombers; the weary refugees with their salvaged household possessions; family members searching for each other; 'demoralisation' and the question of morale; the unfeeling detachment of the raiders (implied by words like 'systematic' and 'tactics'), the cruelty of those tactics, especially in killing women, children, priests and livestock; and the purpose of the raid as first to 'stampede' the population and then to bomb the shelters. Both Monks and Steer talk about the killing of sheep, which takes on a metaphorical Christian resonance, especially in the context of the stoical heroism of the clergy. These were ideas and images that for the next two years would recur visually in propaganda posters, photographs and paintings (not least Picasso's), and in leaflets, speeches, books, poems like Paul Eluard's 'La Victoire de Guernica' ('The Victory of Guernica', 1937) which, in 1949, along with Picasso's painting, became the basis of a short film by Alain Resnais, novels like Hermann Kesten's *Die Kinder von Guernica* (*Children of Guernica*), and plays. For example, their influence can be seen in Barrie Stavis's short play *Refuge* (1938), written for performance by left-wing theatre groups, or in verse plays written for the new medium of radio, like the American writer Norman Corwin's *They Fly Through the Air With the Greatest of Ease*, which was broadcast by CBS in February 1939. Archibald MacLeish's earlier verse play for American radio, *Air Raid* (1938), builds towards the death of a group of women (the most horrific pictures in the newspapers had been pictures of women trying to escape the bombing at Guernica – something which struck Picasso very forcibly as he worked on his painting). Most famously, these were ideas that animated the panic response to Orson Welles's radio production of *War of the Worlds* in October 1938.

The Basque interior minister, Telesforo Monzon, wrote a defiant poem simply called 'Gernika', which is almost an eye-witness account itself, and which adds the tree of Gernika to the store of images in an attempt to quarry renewed Basque strength out of anger:

> Gernika is burning, aflame!
> At night, high Vizcaya appeared to us
> buried in blood,
> and among the stones we had
> a village on live coals.
>
> Hard to believe, I have arrived
> at Gernika in the middle of the night:
> the village is burning, aflame!
> Children sleep on the roads.
> The brother looks for his brother
> and the father finds his murdered son!
> Cows bellow in the wilderness ...
> A woman with no tears in her eyes.
>
> Listen, listen to the noise of the flames.
> The blood-teardrop looks like lightning,
> but the invader fights for nothing:
> the Tree resists, standing with its arms wide open.
> If Gernika belonged to us,
> now the Earth has what belonged to her.
> Gernika has united
> in the name of freedom! ...

By contrast, another Basque poet, Mikel Zarate, writing later, drew more on the dislocations of Picasso's painting than on the event itself in his poem '1937, Apirilak 26' ('26 April 1937')

> An insane instruction, a demonstration of strength.
> The dance of the winged bull's bellowing.
> Hell comes into our skies,
> with the speed of a thunderbolt,
> intense in its anger, towards Gernika ...
> The town's annihilation begun, already begun,
> and affliction already cries.
> The mother, the son, scream their heads off
> by the father's headless body;
> the bird screams, the cock screams, steel screams.
> Stone, flesh, and boiling fire,
> the people's eternal shame screams
> the eternal cry of freedom.

Guernica became a landmark in history, around which crystallised many of the previously disparate fears connected with technology and air warfare. 'From now on,' wrote the journalist Luigi Sturzo in late May or June 1937, 'the history of future wars, in speaking of aerial bombings, will refer to Guernica as one now refers to the *Lusitania*, in speaking of torpedoing by submarines.' From this point on, Guernica became a cultural symbol. Not just Picasso's painting, which acted in a way as a symbol of that symbol, but the very word 'Guernica' itself carried an accumulation of horror at everything connected with the bombing of undefended civilian towns and homes.

Steer's report appeared in *The Times* and the *New York Times* on 28 April. It was not the only report of the bombing that day: there were Noel Monks's in the *Daily Express*, a Reuters dispatch in the *Glasgow Herald*, the *Manchester Guardian* and the *Daily Herald* (which also carried an unsigned dispatch from Bilbao), a cable from Elizabeth Wilkinson in the *Daily Worker*, and reports in normally pro-Nationalist newspapers like the *Morning Post*, the *Daily Telegraph* and the *Daily Mail*. The immediate response from the Nationalists to Aguirre's statement on Radio Bilbao was extremely shrill. 'Mentiras, mentiras, mentiras' ('Lies, lies, lies') was how the radio broadcast from Salamanca began on the evening of 27 April. 'Aguirre lies! He lies basely. In the first place, there is no German or foreign air force in Nationalist Spain … In the second place, we did not bomb Guernica. Franco's Spain does not set fires.' 'Red' incendiarists were to blame. And anyway, the statement concluded, 'Our planes, because of bad weather, have not been able to fly today.' (The bombing had, of course, taken place on the previous day, which was a perfect, clear, late-spring day.) It might seem that lies as transparent as these would have had a short shelf-life and little long-term effect, but that was not the case. Luis Bolín, the head of Franco's press office, was a bullying, controlling and determined personality, who rigorously controlled the content of all foreign press transmissions. He was aided by the many abroad who wanted not to believe the truth of Guernica, who wanted to continue thinking (however improbably) of Franco as a gallant Christian gentleman, defending civilisation and the true faith from Communist atheists and the approaching dark. The Vatican, too, gave all the support it could to Bolín's version of events. The Germans denied all involvement.

One consequence of the controversy was to polarise left-

and right-wing journalism and undermine appeasement by revealing the nature of the German involvement in Spain. The lies enumerated by Herbert Southworth in his book are staggering, though not of course restricted to this incident. In November 1938, towards the end of the conflict, George Orwell complained that 'the atmosphere of lies that surrounds every aspect of [the Spanish struggle] is suffocating'. Southworth also points out that the lies were seldom the work of newspaper journalists, but came from the pens of 'more pliable' writers. Among these were Arnold Lunn, Douglas Jerrold (who certainly knew the truth and consciously distorted it), the Marqués de Moral and Charles Grey (a fascist sympathiser, and editor of *The Aeroplane*). Nigel Tangye – pilot, aeronautical engineer, aviation writer and ardent supporter of Franco – cynically described the Condor Legion as 'an organisation which is formed by German volunteers for mechanical units', and it is common to find the claim that the only Germans in Nationalist Spain were 'technicians'. Only rarely does the smooth surface of untruth get dented. The *Sunday Times* journalist Virginia Cowle famously described an incident in October, almost six months after the bombing, in which a Franco press officer, Ignacio Rosalles, was talking about Guernica. '"The town was full of Reds," he said. "They tried to tell us it was bombed, not burnt." The tall staff officer replied: "But, of course, it was bombed. We bombed it and bombed it and bombed it, and *bueno*, why not?" Rosalles looked astonished, and when we were back in the car again heading for Bilbao, he said: "I don't think I would write about that if I were you."' (She did send her story in, and it was printed on 17 October.)

Writing in the July 1937 issue of *The Criterion*, T. S. Eliot's tone is typical of those who were unwilling to accept that apparent exaggeration could be the truth, even when used for left-wing propaganda purposes. He wrote:

> The situation in Spain has provided the perfect opportunity for extremists of both extremes. To turn from the shrill manifestoes of the Extreme Left, and the indiscretions of the Dean of Canterbury, to the affirmations of Mr. Jerrold and Mr. Lunn, is only to intensify the nightmare. On the First of May, *The Tablet* provided its explanation of the destruction of Guernica: the most likely culprits, according to *The Tablet*, were the Basques' own allies, their shady friends in Catalonia.

The measured distance this has to take from left-wing shrillness, the implication that *The Tablet* had reached a considered opinion based on credible evidence, the relief at its 'explanation', and the use of the phrase 'shady friends' to suggest duplicity on the part of the Catalonian anarchists – all these are characteristic of the distaste with which a certain, powerful, section of British society viewed the bombing. At least we have the benefit of the indefatigable work that Herbert Southworth carried through to establish exactly what took place. In his exhaustive book, all lies are followed back to their source, and fully assessed, so that wherever possible readers can see who told what to whom, what censorship occurred, where, and why.

The contemporary and later eyewitness accounts of the destruction of Guernica seem almost naively surprised as we read them today. Many of them reiterate the same experience through different eyes: collapsing buildings, smoke and fire, panic, lost children or mothers or relatives, dead bodies or severed parts of bodies, the cries of the injured.

Each experience is personal, and each victim is unable to understand why this should have happened to them. As they were told and retold in the world press, these accounts gathered headlines and commentary and became ammunition in a secondary but longer-lasting war of words. Contradictions abounded, so that for much of the debate the personal testimony of witnesses and victims was disbelieved or disregarded in favour of the larger picture, with people being ready to believe one side of the argument or the other before examining the evidence. The physical evidence, anyway, was subject to controversy. The right-wing view, propagated vigorously for example in a hefty English pamphlet called *Guernica. The Official Report of the Commission appointed by the Spanish National Government to investigate the causes of the Destruction of Guernica on April 26–28*, which printed twenty-eight photographs and twenty-four signed eyewitness reports, acknowledged some bombing, but attributed most of the destruction to fires set by the 'Reds'. People on the whole believed what they wanted to believe.

Many attacks since then, including the ones we have grown used to seeing in Iraq and the Middle East in recent years, have been on such a scale that Guernica's fate seems almost insignificant by comparison. But it's almost impossible to overestimate the outrage it caused in 1937. George Steer's report in *The Times* was the main source of information to begin with, and this was enough to prompt heated debate in the British parliament on 28 and 29 April. Sir Archibald Sinclair, leader of the twenty Liberal MPs, spoke for many when he called it 'a deliberate attempt to use air power as an instrument of massacre and terrorism'. It was this aspect which struck the most resonant chord with the public in Europe and America, for reasons which will become clearer in the next chapter. The assault on Guernica came in the middle of a row about the naval blockade of Bilbao, in which the Admiralty was almost openly siding with Franco and forbidding British merchant ships to enter Bilbao's waters, and the focus on the legalities of that issue partly overshadowed the larger political issues at stake. But the horror of Guernica, and the prospect that it might be repeated at Bilbao, put additional pressure on the government to send naval vessels to help evacuate residents and refugees. The official position was cautious and politic. It was summed up in a statement from the Foreign Secretary, Sir Anthony Eden: that Her Majesty's government 'deplore the bombardment of the civilian population in the Spanish Civil War, wherever it may occur and whoever may be responsible'. All through the debate right-wingers like Captain Victor Cazalet kept jumping up to reiterate the Nationalist point of view.

The debate in the House of Lords the following day (29 April) allowed for longer speeches. Viscount Cecil called for a 'most serious and energetic protest' from the government. The attack on Guernica was unprecedented and 'simply designed as an act of terrorism'. If the reports about it were true, he said, 'this is one of the most horrible things that has ever been done'. The simple language is eloquent. Lord Strabolgi reminded the House that, 'whatever we may be told about the rest of the population of Spain, the Basques are a very pious, ancient, courageous and altogether an admirable people … They helped us when we needed help in the Great War.' Lord Plymouth temporised for the government: there was 'no official information'; he was 'not in a position to confirm or deny'; the government would 'continue to examine the problem [of the bombardment of civilians] from every angle'.

The British weekly magazine *The Listener* in the week after the event carried two eloquent photographs on its picture page: an image of the peaceful market town of Guernica, hills receding into the distance behind the houses, with the nearest houses reflected in still water in the foreground, was accompanied by a second shot, this time of silent, empty ruins. There was little follow-up to it, however. The weeks that followed the bombing were more taken up with the coronation of King George VI, and with the *Hindenburg* airship disaster. In *Life and Letters Today*, in 1937 a quarterly publication, an editorial contrasted children who were given special access to watch the coronation procession with the four thousand Basque refugee children who arrived at the same time. It had been suggested that the coronation would make a major impression on the children who saw it, who would then be able to tell their children and grandchildren about it, ensuring (I suppose) some sort of continuity of support for the monarchy. 'These Basque children,' the editorial went on,

> are also a generation that will hand on their impression to the next. With them, it will be of débris, not decoration; aerial bombs instead of 'pennies from heaven', and searchlight and shellfire rather than illuminations. These young Basques have been given war by their elders. They have partaken, against their will, of that worst of man's achievements – not only the destruction of life, but the belittling of it in men's minds.

Accounts of the bombing were widely printed in the American press, and provoked a great deal of anger and indignation in most quarters, although the counter-

5. Guernica after the bombardment.

information strategy which was working well in Europe – especially in France – was soon set in motion in America too. The *New York Times*, which printed Steer's reports, echoed their sentiments in three editorials, and the *Herald Tribune* and *New York Post* also carried stories sympathetic to the Basques. The US ambassador to Spain, Claude Bowers, cabled Washington on 30 April: 'Guernica "holy city" of the Basques totally destroyed though an open country town with unarmed population by huge bombs dropped from insurgent planes of German origin and pilotage ... Denials by insurgents and Germany following world reaction incredible.' Incredible they may have been, but the denials were repeated frequently, especially in the conservative Catholic press and in other newspapers influenced by the need to retain the Catholic vote or to support existing US investment in Spain. (ITT and Texaco, for instance, provided substantial communications and fuel aid to Franco on extended credit.) The editor of the Catholic magazine *America* called the bombing of Guernica 'the greatest propaganda hoax', and Father Joseph F. Thorning, a Jesuit historian and professor of sociology at Mount St Mary's College in Maryland, and a well-known lobbyist for Franco, told an American Catholic Historical Association meeting that any damage done by bombing was 'insignificant in comparison with the havoc perpetrated by gasoline flames kindled by Spanish anarchists in their retreat'. The line about anarchists comes up time and again, prompted by Franco's press officers, regardless of the fact that the Basques were not anarchists but Christian nationalists, who sided with the Republic in pursuit of their full independence from Spain. However, nothing prompted intervention from the American government, which stuck to what Hugh Thomas calls a policy of 'timid and indolent isolation'.

Of the local Basque accounts, the one which made the greatest impression at the time came from a Catholic priest, Father Alberto de Onaindia, a canon of Valladolid cathedral, who happened to be in Guernica by chance when the bombing started. This is how he described what happened to him in his memoirs, published much later, in 1973, but reiterating the things he said in interviews at the time:

It was about quarter past four in the afternoon when we reached the Foral Town [as Guernica was known]. It was Monday, and market day. We were just going past the station when we heard a bomb explode, followed immediately by two more. An aeroplane flying very low dropped its load and was gone in just a few seconds. It was Guernica's first experience of war. The panic of those first moments shook the local population and the country-dwellers who had come in to the weekly market. We were aware of a buzz of excitement and fear. We got out of the car and tried to find out what was happening and to calm down the many women who were clearly nervous and upset. Minutes later more bombs fell in the area around the Convent de las Madres Mercedarias, and people began to leave the streets and hide in shelters, basements or any other cover they could find. Almost at once about eight heavy planes appeared, as if they were coming from the sea, which dropped large numbers of bombs, and behind them followed a veritable rain of incendiary bombs. For more than three hours wave after wave of bombers came, and planes with incendiary bombs, and single machines that came down to a height of about 200 metres to machine-gun the poor people who were fleeing in terror. I do not know what kind of aeroplanes they were, because I do not know anything about that sort of thing. For a long time we remained at the edge of the town, by the road to Munitibar and Marquina. The bursting of the bombs, the fires that were starting to break out and the harassment of the machine-gunning planes forced us to take cover under trees, or the porches of houses, and to throw ourselves flat when we were on open ground and saw a plane approaching. There was no anti-aircraft fire at all, nor any defences, we were hemmed in and surrounded by diabolical forces who were chasing thousands of defenceless inhabitants. Animals from the market, donkeys, pigs and chickens, were running loose in the streets. In the middle of the conflagration we saw people screaming, praying or gesticulating at the aeroplanes. We finally left the town, which was burning, but seeing a number of planes coming straight towards us, we abandoned the car and ran to take cover under the trees. There was a stream there, with a small stone bridge, and we sheltered beneath it while three bombs exploded a few metres away, raising a cloud of dust that blinded us. Some people left the road and climbed the few metres into the woods. When calm returned, we discovered one woman dead, machine-gunned, and a young *gudari* who had been killed by the blast. He did not have any injuries, but a lot of blood was running from his mouth and his nose. I gave them both absolution. We were told that the *gudari* was called Gotzon. All the culverts and ditches were full of people trying to hide or shelter from the cowardly attack of the enemy aeroplanes. Providence saved us that day. Lots of tree branches and quantities of earth fell on our heads every time bombs exploded near us. At a quarter to eight on that glorious April evening the systematic destruction of our sacred town ended.

In Bilbao the next day he described what he'd seen at Guernica to President Aguirre, who sent him to France to publicise it. What happened to his testimony after that makes a useful and symptomatic case study. Several interviews appeared in the press in Belgium, France and England, and provoked a certain amount of comment and controversy. His account of events was almost the only accurate one to appear in the French press, which mostly supported the Franco version. Southworth observes that 'Paris was the only capital in the Western world with a free press where the readers of the large-circulation newspapers were told nothing about a significant development in the story of the destruction of Guernica.' The Havas news agency failed to distribute the interview with Father Onaindia. It was reprinted, with the accounts of Steer and Monks, and four Guernica nurses, in the liberal journal *Esprit* in June, along with other documents from both sides. The eyewitness accounts were followed by the various contradictory denials and a precis of the many fabricated newspaper stories about 'Red' incendiarists, and left no room for doubt about where the truth really lay. The whole twenty-five page section was captioned 'Guernica or the technique of lying', and was prefaced by the famous quotation from *Mein Kampf* where Hitler argues that a big lie is more effective than a small one, and more likely to be believed than the truth.

As soon as Father Onaindia's first interview was printed, a concerted campaign began work to discredit him and his testimony. The attacks were intensified when he managed to send a version of his eyewitness statement to the Vatican, as a protest against the bombing of innocent Christian Basques. The *New York Times* described him as 'just an unfrocked young priest', and General Queipo de Llano, Franco's leading broadcaster, endorsed this in material he sent to the *Catholic Herald* in London and to *L'Action française*, adding that Onaindia had already been excommunicated by the Pope. This story was repeated in the London Catholic weekly *The Universe*, and in the *Catholic Times*. In *L'Action française*, the journalist Charles Maurras (writing from prison, where he was serving eight months for incitement to murder Léon Blum and 100 other deputies) gleefully dismissed Onaindia's evidence. 'The fable, the twice-odious fable, has been disproved. Guernica was not destroyed by the National air force. The town did not perish under the bombs dropped from the sky. It was devoured by the fires which the Russians methodically set on leaving the town.'

In Maurras's bizarrely unhinged paranoid universe, it was not merely Republicans or 'Reds' who set fire to Guernica, but actual Russians. In France, it was the socialists, Jews and homosexuals who were to blame for this 'enterprise of falsification'. Not all Catholics lined up behind Franco, however. On 8 May another section of the French Catholic population made its opinion known: a document appeared in several Catholic newspapers, signed by François Mauriac, Gabriel Marcel, Jacques Maritain, Maurice Merleau-Ponty and dozens of other important intellectual figures, supporting the eyewitness account of Father Onaindia.

> The Spanish Civil War has just taken on, in the Basque country, a particularly atrocious appearance. Yesterday, it was the aerial bombardment of Durango. Today, by the same method, it is the almost complete destruction of Guernica, a town without defence, sanctuary of Basque traditions. Hundreds of non-combatants, of women and children, have perished at Durango, at Guernica and elsewhere ... Nothing justifies, nothing excuses, the bombing of open towns such as Guernica.

But in 1937 Pope Pius XI and his aides were concerned more with supporting those who upheld the Church than with establishing the truth about individual events. The argument rapidly produced two opposing camps: those for whom the Catholic Church and its supporters must always be in the right, which included the Vatican and the Duke of Alba and his English propaganda movement, the Friends of Nationalist Spain, who denied that Guernica had been bombed; and those who, like Jacques Maritain, Georges

Bernanos and other more open-minded Catholics, set mortal and humanitarian considerations, and objective truth, above politics and ideology.

One other eyewitness account may be cited here. On 30 April, four days after the bombing of Guernica, the commander of the Condor Legion, Wolfram von Richthofen, wrote a dispassionate account in his diary of what he'd seen that day when he flew low over the ruins of the town, and the partially destroyed towns of Verriz, Guerricaiz and Durango.

Guernica, town of 5000 inhabitants, literally razed to the ground. Attack carried out with 250-kilogram and incendiary bombs, the latter making up about 1/3. When the I. Jus. came, there was already dense smoke everywhere (from the VB, which attacked with 3 planes), nobody could make out streets, bridge or targets on the edge of town so they just dropped everything wherever they could. The 250-kgs knocked down a quantity of houses and destroyed the water supply. So the incendiary bombs had time to spread and work effectively. The construction of the houses – tiled roofs, wooden galleries and half-timbering – resulted in complete annihilation. Inhabitants were mostly outdoors because of the holiday, a number of others left the town just as [the bombing] began. A small number died in air-raid shelters when they were hit. – Bomb craters still visible in the streets, fantastic. – Town was completely cut off for at least 24 hours, which would have made for total success if only troops had been moved up there. As it was, just a complete technical success for our 250s and the EC.B.1s [incendiaries] … Sacred oak tree in Guernica, beneath which for over a thousand years (old trunk under glass, new tree planted) the constitution and laws of Vizcaya were made. Beside that, a church and parliament. Nothing destroyed at all in the district at the edge of the town.

Richthofen is pleased with the success of his military experiment. Nothing else enters the equation. It is clear that he has little knowledge of the symbolic importance of Guernica, but that it is also unlikely that knowledge of it would have done anything to alter his military objective. It might even have made the town a more desirable target. As it is, his terse, technocratic narrative touches on several crucial matters without ever attempting to enlarge or comment on any of them. The threefold nature of the raid, the incomplete military value of the attack, the size, age and situation of the town, and Guernica's unique significance in Basque society are all mentioned, but in the most disinterested way imaginable. All of them, however, are of central importance to the myth and counter-myth of Guernica.

THE ROLE OF THE CONDOR LEGION

At this point it may be as well to clarify the position of these German airmen in northern Spain. How did they come to be involved? After launching his rebellion, one of Franco's first acts, on 22 July, was to send envoys to Germany to ask for military support. After various misadventures, these messengers finally met Hitler at Bayreuth on the evening of 26 July. Hitler immediately agreed to provide as much aid as was necessary, and ordered Göring to organise it. Four days later, men and machines were on their way to Spanish Morocco, where some thirty thousand of the toughest troops in the Spanish army were garrisoned. By sending a fleet of twenty Junkers Ju-52 transport planes, Hitler was able to help Franco move over twenty thousand soldiers from North Africa to Seville. The Luftwaffe transported two-thirds of them, along with some 270 tonnes of military equipment, and almost certainly saved the rebel forces from defeat in the summer of 1936. The operation demonstrated convincingly and for the first time that, in war, aircraft were not merely useful for dropping bombs: the airlift brought a new and crucial kind of mobility.

Nazi Germany was not deeply interested in the Spanish Civil War, but Hitler did not want to see a Soviet-assisted victory in the Mediterranean (the Soviet Union also sent a large quantity of men and up-to-date weaponry to help the Republicans). He also wanted access to Spain's minerals, especially the high-quality iron ore (haematite) from the Basque country, mercury, wolfram and pyrites, all of which were necessary for the German armaments industry. Spain would also be a valuable experimental testing ground for new aircraft and new techniques. So in the autumn of 1936 the size of the German contingent in Spain was increased to about five thousand, mostly Luftwaffe volunteers, with about a hundred more aircraft. The new force was christened the Condor Legion, and, apart from the staff, consisted of three to four bomber squadrons (K/88), the same number of fighter squadrons (J/88), two squadrons of reconnaissance planes (A/88), and one squadron of seaplanes (AS/88), with all the necessary support in the way of communications, logistics and medical battalions. There was also one battalion of anti-aircraft batteries, and two experimental groups for trial combat-testing the newest aircraft models (VJ/88 for fighters, VB/88 for bombers). The commander of the

Condor Legion was Lieutenant-Colonel Wolfram Freiherr von Richthofen, a cousin of the First World War 'Red Baron' and a former air attaché in Rome. A fluent Italian-speaker, he now rapidly learned Spanish too. The Condor Legion's first major assignment came in the autumn of 1936, in attacks on Madrid. That was where it developed the technique of flying in successive waves of bombers, with the first wave dropping the largest bombs, up to 1,000 kg, to destroy large buildings, then a second wave bringing smaller bombs to further break up the damage caused by the first wave, and finally a wave of incendiaries to start fires and of anti-personnel bombs to kill the people who tried to put them out. Madrid had been proving a difficult target, the Republic's Soviet fighters superior to Franco's German and Italian fighters, and by November it was clear that things there were going the way of the Republicans. In an attempt to move forward, the Nationalist forces started a bombing campaign, which did a lot of damage and inflicted major casualties (on 30 November, 244 civilians were killed and 875 wounded) but had almost no visible effect on morale. In fact if any morale suffered, it was that of the Nationalists, who were forced to fly only in large formations with heavy fighter escorts.

While the Madrid front was at stalemate, the situation in the Basque country, where much of the nation's mineral wealth lay, was very different. The Nationalists' capture of San Sebastián in the previous September had effectively cut the Basque country off from the rest of Spain. Now the Republicans there were encircled and vulnerable to an offensive. The demonstration of air power and coordinated air and ground tactics that had enabled the Republicans to defeat the Italians at Guadalajara showed how vulnerable ground troops could be to aircraft attack, and both the Condor Legion commanders and the Franco government saw the terrain in Vizcaya as suited to this sort of warfare. In March 1937 the Legion was redeployed to the airfields at Vitoria and Burgos (with the bombers at the latter) and given overall control of the air operation in the north. This gave it a combined force of some 150 aircraft against the small handful of planes at the disposal of the Basques. Ten fighters were sent to the Basques from Valencia, flying over Nationalist-held country. Only seven made it, and no more were sent. There were additional reasons why the Republican commanders were reluctant to commit planes and artillery to support the Basques: the war in the north was, ultimately, less important than the survival of Madrid and central Spain; and there was also a sense that the Basques, with their insistence on independence, should fight their own battles. With so little opposition, this would be, in James Corum's words, 'the Luftwaffe's first major opportunity to show what a modern air force could achieve in combat'.

General Emilio Mola, one of the generals central to Franco's rise to power, and now commander of the Ejercito del Norde (Army of the North), began the campaign on 31 March with a threat in a 'proclamation to the people of Euskadi', printed in leaflets dropped (as if they were warnings of the bombs to come) from the air on to the main towns of the region. 'I have decided to put a speedy end to the war in the north,' they read. 'The lives and property of those who surrender with their arms and who are not guilty of murder will be respected. But if submission is not immediate, I shall raze Vizcaya to the ground, beginning with the war industry. I have the means to do so.' As if to show that Mola meant business, in a terrifying demonstration of the power of aerial bombing, the Condor Legion attacked Durango, 'the first defenceless town to be mercilessly bombed', as Hugh Thomas put it. A pattern was set by Franco's resident liar, General Queipo de Llano, on Seville radio, when he claimed that the bombing had been of 'military objectives', and that Communists had locked the priest and congregation in the church and set it on fire. The same version of events was repeated on Radio Valladolid on 2 April.

The Condor Legion planes were meant to be supporting the ground offensive, but Mola was irritatingly cautious in the way he conducted the operation. All through April, the German fliers under Richthofen's command were frustrated. They kept on flying out to prepare the way for ground troop movements, bombing and strafing government positions, and sustaining damage and losses, only to discover that the Spanish and Italian troops were not planning an offensive that day, or if they were that they had only limited objectives. This allowed the Basque army time to regroup and organise its retreat, rather than being scattered and destroyed once and for all. A German report described the Spanish officers as 'lazy, stupid, unwilling to learn and arrogant. They are a hindrance.' However, a new Nationalist advance began on 20 April, and was quickly effective. On 25 April the Basque troops started to fall back from Marquina to form a new front before Guernica. Guernica was not in itself a prime military target on 26 April, but it could be said to have occupied an important position for the retreating Basque forces, being situated at the head of the estuary, at an important crossroads and bridge; but neither the bridge nor the road to it was damaged in the bombing. And, anyway, saturation bombing followed by incendiaries is not a recommended or an effective method of attacking stone bridges.

In the aftermath of the bombing of Guernica, Mola broadcast the following statement over the radio, as reported in the *Daily Herald* on 29 April 1937. 'We shall raze Bilbao to the ground and its bare, desolate site will remove the British desire to support the Basque Bolsheviks, against our will. We must destroy the capital of a perverted people, who dares defy the irresistible cause of the national idea.' Having already destroyed the symbolic capital of the 'perverted' Basques, Mola had shown the force of his words. Guernica was only the ceremonial centre of Basque government – all the administrative and government offices were in Bilbao. As Steer put it, 'Bilbao was trembling.' The Spanish and Italian forces, and their German advisers, were very keen to avoid the kind of siege that had been bogging down forces round Madrid since the previous November. Guernica had succeeded in its aim of showing what Franco's forces, or at least the Condor Legion, were capable of.

The combination of air support and ground offensive gradually drove the Basque forces back, and by early June they had retreated to positions behind the defensive fortifications, trenches and concrete pillboxes which made up the *cinturón*, or 'iron ring', that encircled Bilbao and the surrounding area. Steady progress had been made during May. By 13 June all the Basque troops had been withdrawn within the iron ring. The insurgent forces were six miles from Bilbao – within shelling distance of it. A decision was taken to evacuate civilians from the city, to Santander; predictably, the road to Santander was machine-gunned by the Condor Legion on 14 June. The army would continue to defend Bilbao. (However, as Hugh Thomas has pointed out, evacuating cities makes them harder to defend, as the defending forces are no longer fighting for their homes and families.)

Colonel Joseph Putz, formerly the commander of the XIV International Brigade, took over command of the 1st Basque Division on 14 June, and on the following day he succeeded in re-establishing a line of defence. But this was quickly broken, thanks to information given to the Nationalists by a defector, Captain Goicoechea, the officer who had been in charge of the construction of the defences. He had driven his car over to the Nationalist side in early March, and had taken with him all the plans and a detailed knowledge of all the weak spots. On 19 June a combination of that treachery, very heavy bombing and the threat to destroy Bilbao in the same way as Durango and Guernica had been destroyed finally brought about the surrender of Bilbao, and shortly afterwards the Basque defeat.

For the Luftwaffe, the Spanish Civil War was a laboratory in which to test its machines and techniques, and put theory into practice. One of the tenets that Richthofen had learned in Italy from the writings of the pioneer of total air warfare, Giulio Douhet, and his followers was the importance of using bombing to destroy both the military and the civilian morale of the enemy. In one of the entries in his diary, Richthofen wrote, 'Fear, which cannot be stimulated in peaceful training of troops, is very important, because it affects morale. Morale is more important in winning battles than weapons. Continuously repeated, concentrated air attacks have the most effect on the morale of the enemy.' This was the thinking behind the attacks on Durango and Guernica and the other towns lying just behind the front lines. It also underlay the attack during the night of 24 April, when a squadron of Ju-52s attacked the explosives factory in Galdacano, the industrial centre of Bilbao, where the Basque military headquarters was also situated. The sheer size and loudness of the explosions as the stores of dynamite went up was intended to cause the maximum amount of fear and apprehension – what these days is called 'shock and awe'. Corum claims that 'it is no exaggeration to say that the Condor Legion made the Nationalist victory in the north possible ... Air power in northern Spain in 1937 not only proved that it had great shock and destructive effects, but also proved that the side possessing air superiority would hold the initiative on the battlefield.' One of the ways in which air superiority was henceforth to be sought and demonstrated was by acts of total war like the bombing of Guernica.

GUERNICA IN THE CIVIL WAR

The response to the tragedy of Guernica in the outside world was inextricable from the response to the Spanish Civil War itself, which had at this point been going on for over nine months. It was a profoundly complex conflict presented as a melodramatically simple one. Most of those outside Spain had no idea of the forces at work within the country, but were more than ready to interpret them as part of the struggle between Left and Right, socialism and barbarism, tyranny and freedom which provided the melodramatic backdrop to so many world events from China to France. Those – fewer, but still vocal and influential – who saw the civil war as a battle between Catholicism and Communism still saw the same dichotomy at work, with the difference that the Communists were the barbarians and the enemies of peace and progress. But the struggle over the future direction of Spanish life had a real, human dimension at the same time as the melodramatic one, as George Orwell felt immediately on his arrival in Republican Barcelona: 'It was the first time that I had ever been in a town where the working class was in the saddle ... Waiters and shop-walkers looked you in the face and treated you as an equal. Servile and even ceremonial forms of speech had temporarily disappeared ... There was much in it that I did not understand, in some ways I did not even like it, but I recognised it immediately as a state of affairs worth fighting for.' Anarchist Catalonia was very different from the Basque province of Vizcaya, as it was from Madrid, but in all those places there was a deeply felt need to fight for what was perceived as freedom, and against an illegal military uprising.

Spain was widely, and not entirely inaccurately, regarded as a pre-modern society, riddled with feudal institutions and traditions: the British Cabinet minutes for December 1936, for instance, show the Foreign Office arguing that conditions in Spain were more like those in a Central or South American state than a European one. The Austrian sociologist Franz Borkenau concluded his 1937 book *The Spanish Cockpit* with the observation that one of the lures or attractions of Spain was that 'it was a civilisation near to ourselves, closely connected with the historical past of Europe, but which has not participated in our later developments towards mechanism, the adoration of quantity, and of the utilitarian aspect of things'. The industrialised areas of the Basque country would have to be excluded from this account, but with that proviso we can read on:

In this lure exerted by Spain is implied the concession, unconscious very often, it is true, that after all something seems to be wrong with our own civilisation and that the backward, stagnant, and inefficient Spaniard can well compete, in the field of human values, with the efficient, practical and progressive European. The one seems pre-destined to last, unmoving, throughout the cataclysms of the surrounding world, and to outlive national usurp-ers and foreign conquerors; the other, progressive, may progress towards his own destruction.

This argument is right, I think, and enabled the bombing of Guernica to take on the significance it did. It gave tangible and comprehensible form to something not quite express-ible but still felt by many people about bombing as it was being deployed by colonial powers like France or Britain. The innocent people of Guernica, with their strong family structures and rural market, coupled with their very old democratic tradition, made the town a bridge between the exotic unreality of the 'native' villages bombed into submis-sion by the RAF and the pressing ordinariness of life in an English city, so vulnerable to attack from the air.

In Britain, the popular image of Spain was further dis-torted by the popular history of Anglo-Spanish relations over the past three hundred and fifty years: the role of the Armada and the Elizabethan war with Spain were an important and picturesque part of Our Island Story, as were stories of the brutality of the Inquisition. The Spanish Empire had declined as the British Empire grew during the eighteenth century, and the legacy of the Peninsular war and the Carlist wars only reinforced the sense of a politi-cally unstable, socially backward country. In reality it was a country with a great deal of British investment: in 1923, direct investment in Spain was probably worth over £40 million; by the time the civil war broke out, in July 1936, despite expropriations and the unsettled political situation of recent years, British capital worth considerably more than that was deployed in Spain, with the mining company Rio Tinto being the largest investor. An important source of supply for the armaments industry, Rio Tinto had the world's largest open-cast copper mine at Huelva. British companies were modernising railways, building electric lighting systems, and carrying out other similar works in Spain. In 1923 the American firm ITT won the contract to renew the entire Spanish telephone network, creating assets for itself worth $90 million by 1929. And Spain had been becoming an increasingly important trading partner. All these factors led the Foreign Office and the British government to favour any strong government which held out the promise of suppressing strikes, sit-ins and nationalisation, however authoritarian it might be. They wanted, as in all other areas of foreign policy since 1917, to combat Soviet Communist influence, which they tended to detect in any movement towards democratisation and workers' rights. These facts, however, were not what the media concentrated on: they preferred to evoke a more picturesque Spain – a land of bright colours, quaint customs, sherry, gypsies, bullfights, flamenco, passion, feuds, sunlight, aridity and Don Quixote: the sort of place you might expect something as exotic as a civil war to break out.

The great powers' policy of non-intervention in the civil war was a largely spurious tactic which suited their international diplomacy and aided their commercial interests. As John Stuart Mill had written many years earlier, in another context, 'The doctrine of non-intervention, to be a legitimate principle of morality, must be accepted by all governments. The despot must consent to be bound by it as well as the free States. Unless they do, the profession of it by free countries comes to this miserable issue, that the wrong side may help the wrong, but the right must not help the right.' In a situation where the Soviet Union was sending aid to the Republicans, and Mussolini's Italy and Nazi Germany were sending considerably more to Franco, the stubborn refusal of Britain and France to admit as much, or to move an inch from their position of non-intervention, amounted, as was often and justly claimed, to intervention on the side of the insurgents.

While the origins of the civil war lay deep within the tensions and contradictions of Spanish history, its power and resonance in the 1930s stemmed from the way in which these very local concerns were played out in terms of more general, even apparently universal, politics. It was the fourth or fifth civil war to break out in Spain since the Royalist War of 1820–23, and, like the others, it revealed what Paul Preston has called 'a curious pattern in Spain's modern history, arising from a frequent *desfase*, or lack of synchronisation, between the social reality and the political power structure ruling over it'. For almost a hundred years, governments had alternated between enthusiastic or revolutionary attempts to introduce land reforms and moderate some of the extremes of wealth and poverty and reactionary determination to undo the progressive reforms and reassert the status quo. This reflected contradictions within Spain's slow process of industrialisation: large landed estates tyrannised landless labourers; a small industrial bourgeoisie, like the English bourgeoisie in the nineteenth century, emulated the aristocracy and put their money into land, further tightening the screw on the lives of the poorest country people; and there were growing working-class and anarchist movements.

Little of this touched the Basque country, with its banking

and industrial sectors and productive agricultural land, with economic small and medium-sized farms. The Basques had retained their own standpoint throughout the upheavals of the nineteenth century, siding with those forces, notably the Carlists, who promised support for their regional integrity and for their ancient laws. When the civil war broke out, three of the four Basque provinces declared themselves anti-Franco (Navarre supported the rebels), not out of any enthusiastic loyalty to the Republican government, but because, whatever else its faults, the new Republican government had granted them a substantial measure of independence. In August 1936 the bishops of Vitoria and Pamplona promulgated a pastoral letter in which they pronounced that Catholics were not permitted to make common cause with the Republicans. This was immediately discounted by the vicar-general of Bilbao, who cited papal encyclicals against the Nationalist rebellion. No word was forthcoming from Pope Pius XI in the Vatican, so the position remained unresolved.

To understand the adherence of those Basque provinces to the Republican cause, it is necessary to realise that the uneven history of Basque independence from Spain went back centuries, to the time when, in return for the Basques accepting rule from Castile, each king of Spain was required to go to Guernica, stand beneath its ancient symbolic oak tree, and pledge to uphold the *fueros*, the traditional laws and customs of the Basques. (It was because it was the seat of the *fueros* that Guernica was called the 'foral' town.) Originally, justice was dispensed and decisions were made ceremonially beneath the branches of the Guernica oak tree, which became internationally known as a symbol of ancient, democratic freedoms. Wordsworth wrote a sonnet apostrophising

6. *This cartoon from a Spanish newspaper a few days after the bombing shows both the defensive solidarity inspired by the symbolism of Guernica and its oak tree* (Gernikako Arbola) *and at the same time the unequal struggle of clubs against fascist planes and bombs.*

it and the 'Guardians of Biscay's ancient liberty' in 1810, during the Peninsular War:

Oak of Guernica! Tree of holier power
Than that which in Dodona did enshrine
(So faith too fondly deemed) a voice divine
Heard from the depths of its aërial bower –
How canst thou flourish at this blighting hour?

In 1826 a grand neoclassical meeting house was erected. The old oak died in 1860 (it was three hundred years old) and was immediately replaced by the tree which still stands there, and which has since become symbolically inseparable from Basque national identity.

Modern Basque nationalism, however, like most other forms of nationalist culture, is a creation of the second half of the nineteenth century. The national song, 'Gernikako Arbola', 'The Tree of Guernica', was written in 1853. By the 1890s, conscious attempts were under way to promote the Basque language, felt to be under threat from immigration, education and other pressures of the modern world. The Basque Nationalist Party was founded at the beginning of the twentieth century, a Basque flag was designed, and the region adopted the name of Euskadi, an invented word derived from 'Euskara', the name of the Basque language. The Basques were on the whole deeply Catholic and anti-Republican. But they were even more deeply anti-Spanish, which is why they supported the government that had given them a degree of autonomy.

In the mid-nineteenth century, a new steel industry developed in Vizcaya. Founded on the recently discovered Bessemer process, which made the production of steel faster and

7. *This picture in the Basque Nationalist newspaper,* Euzkadi, *illustrates the 'victory of love over hate' through the survival intact of the Basque Parliament buildings and the Tree of Liberty, the Guernica Oak.*

cheaper, the industry rapidly became a success. The process required haematite, so railways soon linked the haematite mines with Bilbao on the coast. Oil refineries followed, and chemical factories. It was the Basques who created the first industrial bourgeoisie in Spain, with bankers, insurance companies, energy companies and exporters. Most of the iron ore was being sent to Britain, which became a source of friction: under the *fueros*, the export of Vizcayan iron had been forbidden, and some regarded it as indicative of the way in which the region was losing its identity in the search for wealth. It became important in the story of Guernica, however, as many English people in 1937 remembered the bravery of the Basque seamen who had braved German U-boats in the First World War to ensure deliveries of iron ore to Britain. It was this that Lord Strabolgi was referring to in his speech in the House of Lords, quoted on page 39 above. It helped soften opposition to Britain's receiving four thousand Basque children, refugees evacuated from Bilbao in June 1937.

A deep respect for the Basque people animates the whole of Steer's *The Tree of Gernika*, and therefore informs much of the outrage at the bombing of Guernica. C. Day Lewis's long poem 'The Nabara' recounts in verse an episode from Steer's book in which he describes the heroism of the trawler ironically named *Nabara* (Navarre being the only one of the four Basque provinces to declare in favour of Franco) and its fight against the rebel cruiser *Canarias*. Day Lewis's opening lines, 'Freedom is more than a word, more than a base coinage / Of statesmen', become a refrain in the poem. It is repeated near the end, where politicians are condemned for 'hiding behind the skirts of peace / They had defiled' and giving the country up to 'rack and carnage'. 'For these I have told of, freedom was flesh and blood.' Echoes of the British naval tradition add to the sense of solidarity the reader feels with the seamen, of whom only fourteen out of fifty-two survived.

THE AFTERMATH

Spain and Germany had a history when it came to bombing. After defeat in Morocco at the hands of the anti-colonial Berber leader Abd el-Krim in 1923, Spain had been very fierce in its use of bombing there. Motivated by desire for revenge on the short-lived Rif Republic, the Spanish government made a secret deal with Germany for the supply of mustard gas and German expert advisers on its use. Spain disregarded international legal scruples on the use of poison gas, and in December 1923 signed a secret agreement with Germany for the supply of gas-filled artillery shells and aerial bombs. In the winter of 1924–5 the German chemical manufacturer Stolzenberg set up a plant in Spain for the production of mustard-gas bombs and shells, which were to be used in the anti-Rif offensive. That was a slow, destructive campaign, with French forces moving north while Spanish troops pressed south; it was not until May 1926 that Abd el-Krim finally surrendered to the French. During the campaign, as described by Corum and Johnson, 'the Spanish used gas bombs extensively [in] a pure terror campaign that made villages and the civilian population the primary target. [They] preferred to use mustard gas, which tended to blind and cripple rather than kill its victims. Mustard gas, because of its toxicity and persistence, also poisoned and destroyed crops and wells and made life unbearable for the villagers.' They were also happy to use mercenaries. It was volunteer American pilots who destroyed Chechaouen in Morocco.

The joint venture of the Spanish, Italian and German air

forces in the Spanish Civil War brought considerable benefits to all three, just as participation on the other side benefited the Soviet Union. The Luftwaffe in particular developed new techniques, including area bombing and the use of dive-bombers to support ground forces (or just to kill people). After the end of the war it carried out a study of the extensive civil-defence procedures put in place by the Republicans, especially in heavily bombed Madrid. Its observations convinced the German authorities that, as Corum puts it, 'a large-scale civil defence programme could be effective in maintaining civilian morale' – something the British also had to be persuaded of. Wolfram von Richthofen also learned directly from the experience of Guernica. Promoted to field marshal in the Second World War, he oversaw the bombing of Rotterdam, Warsaw, Belgrade, Crete and Stalingrad. The Italians put Douhet's theories into operation in March 1938, when they subjected Barcelona to three days of heavy air bombardment and caused over two thousand casualties in the hope that they would destroy civilian morale. But, rather than weakening morale, the relentlessness of the bombing strengthened it and made the population angrier and more determined. The successful use of air power at Guadalajara persuaded the Soviet commanders to move from an emphasis on heavy bombing to planning for much greater use of air support for ground battles. In all cases, their experience in Spain – including the bombing of Guernica – prepared the way for the air war that was to follow in 1939, and it was the bombings of Madrid, Durango, Barcelona, and most of all Guernica that represented the horrors of war to the civilian populations in other countries.

The controversial and propaganda importance of Guernica has tended to overshadow the bombing of Madrid and Barcelona, and the systematic bombing, from 19 January to 31 March, of the Catalan coast. The official justification for the latter was to prevent the Republicans getting deliveries of material by sea, but there was also a deliberate attempt by the concerted actions of Italian, German and Nationalist Spanish forces to demoralise the Catalans and hasten their surrender. In fact there was so much bombing going on by 1938, and so much had been written about it in the previous twenty years, that the reductive symbolism provided by Guernica, and its shorthand representation in Picasso's painting, was a welcome substitute for the legal, moral, diplomatic and military complexities it raised.

It would be impossible to count, let alone list, all the references to Guernica in the months and years after the bombing. It is generally the case that unprecedented events create a sense that the language available is inadequate for their full description, and this was very markedly the case with Guernica. The reports recycle the same vocabulary until it seems stale and clichéd. Even poems had difficulty finding words equal to the impact of the bombing. Poems were written as an immediate response to the news stories – like Paul Eluard's 'La Victoire de Guernica' (1937), which uses disjunction, fragmentation and obliquity to create its sense of horror – but probably more poems were inspired by Picasso's painting, which he started five days after the bombing, having read the news of it in *L'Humanité*, where it was headlined 'MILLE BOMBES INCENDIAIRES lancées par les avions de Hitler et de Mussolini'. The news story was accompanied by photographs of the dead, and a view of the ruined town. The picture took five weeks to complete, and in its panoramic narrative and monochrome palette it echoed the experience of newsprint, but on a gigantically enlarged scale. Like T. S. Eliot's *The Waste Land* in the realm of poetry, Picasso's painting is a collage of allusion to and quotation from the whole tradition of European art. Works of ancient and modern art that reference the horrors of war, especially Goya's *Third of May* and his *Desastres*, along with more specifically Spanish elements such as the bullfight, are reshaped and put to work within this huge composition. The fragmentary nature of the images, and their characteristic post-Cubist dimensionality, are subordinated to the painting's narrative impact. The painting is dominated by expressive faces, six human, two animal, and most of them are screaming. Picasso's signature gestures and distortions here find their place within a narrative which overflows the pictorial space, so that abstraction works in the service of grief and anger; but then rather than merely reflecting these emotions back into a call to political action, the painting insists on its status as artwork, using the material provided by Guernica, but on its own, formal terms. Its suitability for propaganda purposes rested on the coincidence of Picasso's reputation with the broader significance of the bombing of Guernica: the painting came close to providing a new visual language for such events by virtue of the number of times it was reproduced and the amount of commentary it generated. But the painting itself was unrepeatable. As has often been pointed out, its true heirs were the New York Abstract Expressionists, de Kooning and Motherwell. As a result of it, though, poems like J. F. Hendry's 'Picasso: for Guernica' (1939) helped to create a vocabulary for subsequent work, as for example for Dylan Thomas's poems of the Blitz, or for Hendry's own 1942 book, *The Bombed Happiness*. In this way poems, which had quite a wide circulation on the Left in the late 1930s and an even wider circulation during the first years of the Second World War, began the necessary work of assimilation and comprehension. Bernard Gutteridge's poem 'In September 1939' remembers Spain 'and the black spots / They shouted "Bombers" at. That memory screams / That we know from films or in bad dreams.' Images from newsreel film became familiar from frequent reproduction in newspapers, pamphlets, posters and books, and those images were recycled as words in a cumulative process of assimilation. As a poetic discourse developed, so the scope of the poems deepened to include a broader imagination of bombing, laying the groundwork for the many poems that deal with bombing in the Second World War.

Soon after the attack on Guernica, poignant film of the ruins was shown in British cinemas, notably the Gaumont newsreel released on 6 May, which carried the following powerful commentary: 'First pictures from the Basque Republic of the Holy City of Guernica, scene of the most terrible air raid our modern history can yet boast. Hundreds were killed here, men, women and children. Four thousand bombs were dropped out of a blue sky into a hell that raged unchecked for five murderous hours. This was a city, and these were homes, like yours.' The inaccuracies here – the underestimate of deaths; five hours instead of three or three and a half – are less important than the tone and the appeal to fellow-feeling, and the insistence that all the destruction was carried out from the air. Although the very short film makes no mention of the perpetrators, there is no doubt that it implicitly rejects the Franco line. In Spain, *Guernika* (1937), by architect and film and theatre director Nemesio Sobrevila, used images provided by Aragonese cameraman José María Beltrán. Ivor Montagu's Progressive Film Institute (the PFI) and other UK film-makers produced thirty-two films about the war, including Montagu's *Air Bombardment* (about the bombing of Barcelona) and Basil Wright's documentary on the Basque refugee children, *Children of Spain*.

There were also plenty of powerful photographic images of dead schoolchildren in Madrid and Barcelona to swell the general sense of grief, fear and outrage, and to give rise to further poems such as George Barker's *Calamiterror* and his *Elegy on Spain* (which uses a photo of a dead schoolchild as its frontispiece), and the much-quoted short poem by F. L. Lucas, 'Proud Motherhood (Madrid, A.D. 1937)'. Stanley Richardson's laconic and effective poem 'Air-Raid Over Barcelona' uses the familiar tropes of murder, sacrifice, birds of prey, and death 'sprinkled' from the 'morning skies' on to 'suffering eyelids' (the same photograph of a dead child), and envisages German bombers raining bombs and gas over London. When that day comes, Richardson says, he will not save those 'capitalist chairmen' and non-interventionists who knew what was going on. It remains a powerful poem, even without the knowledge that Richardson himself was killed in a German air raid on London in 1941.

Bombing comes from above; there is no arguing with it; it is no respecter of persons; it destroys individuality; it is fatal, destructive, unemotional and inexorable. As such, it intensifies our sense of the contingency of things and the irrationality of death – especially when that contingency is in the service, as it were, of fascist or other far-right ideologies of power. The Left-liberal humanitarian response to Guernica is part and parcel of the same group's response to the rise of the Right. Civilian bombing in general and Guernica in particular are often described in terms inseparable from this rise. Fear of machines, of non-humanity, of mass production, of obliteration of the individual, of maleness and male oppression, of death rather than life are pitted against traditional ideas of women and children, family, vulnerability, democracy, home, dignity, individuality, culture, art, mutual aid, equality, compassion, suffering, martyrdom and sacrifice. It is a complex web that results.

Hermann Kesten's *Children of Guernica* explores the complexity of the unpredictable relations between states of mind and social attitudes, and the consequences of political indifference in a time of crisis. It tells the story of a Guernica family, half of whom die in the bombing, through the eyes of Carlos, one of the surviving children. The drama is played out through the contrast he ponders between his shallow, frivolous uncle, who survives, and his just, gentle, dead father. Inanity and shallowness are as much responsible for acts like the bombing of Guernica as are pure cruelty, hatred or political vengeance. Like much of the other post-Guernica writing, Kesten's novel is primarily concerned with the question of what constitutes civilisation. And it does that under the shadow of time: the book's ironic epitaph is taken from Beaumarchais, who is given a new, serious, twist. 'Et vive la joie. Qui sait si le monde durera encore trois semaines' ('Enjoy yourselves while you can. Who knows if the world will last another three weeks'). One impact of Guernica was to make the future frightening and close.

Another book which can also deepen our understanding of this sense of the future is Sarah Campion's undeservedly forgotten pacifist novel of ideas *Thirty Million Gas Masks* (1937). At a critical point in it, the central character, Judith, is trying to make a final assessment of the value of her pacifism, as an air raid is about to begin:

> Completely alone, in a dank dark silence, she was face to face with war ... All the gathered up remembered

8. This striking photo shows a woman wearing a gas mask, pushing a pram through bombed out ruins in Berlin in 1945.

terrors of war as a distant menace crowded in on her
mind: atrocity tales from Abyssinia, so many years ago
... Finally Spain – the dragging tortuous horror of it,
the ravaging of Toledo, of Guernica, the papers full of
ghastly pictures, exhibited as curiosities to titillate the
jaded English eye that was bored with mere domestic
murder, rape, and brutalities; the Basque children cowering in a Southampton meadow, cowering away in fear
from the aeroplanes flown thoughtlessly too close by gay
English trippers.

But it is not the horror of war – all the constellated images
of the post-Guernica world – that revolts her so much as
'the horror ... of the English attitude to horror, the wist-
fully benevolent attitude', and the unthinking misery it will
cause. Unable to see a way out, she removes her gas mask as
the gas bombs fall around her.

This too is part of the cultural legacy of Guernica: the
response to the response; the inadequacy of the propaganda,
the uncertainty about the ultimate cause, let alone the ultimate cure, for war. Indeed, the horror of war has a sublimity
about it – and not only in the Futurist fantasies of Marinetti
or in the work of science-fiction writers like H. G. Wells.
Douhet's claim that 'to have command of the air means to
be in a position to wield offensive power so great it defies
human imagination' is an important one. The human imagination has a great deal of work to do in imagining events so
far beyond ordinary civilian experience as the bombing of
Guernica, and there is abundant evidence of poets, writers,
painters and other artists trying to do this, as well as think-
ers, philosophers and politicians.

2

CIVILISATION AND ITS DISCONTENTS

On 10 November 1932, the day before Armistice Day, the House of Commons held a full day's debate on foreign policy, focusing on disarmament and the League of Nations. It was a lively and at times impassioned affair, with much to say about Japan's occupation of Manchuria, and the perils of unilateralism. But aircraft were hardly mentioned, and bombing not at all, until the Lord President of the Council, former prime minister Stanley Baldwin, rose to make the closing speech.

'What the world suffers from,' he announced,

> is a sense of fear, a want of confidence, and it is a fear held instinctively and without knowledge very often. But in my view ... there is no one thing more responsible for that fear – I am speaking now of what the hon. Gentleman for Limehouse [Clement Attlee, who proposed the debate's original motion] called the common people of whom I am chief – there is no greater cause of that fear than the fear of the air ... These feelings exist among ordinary people throughout the whole civilised world, and I doubt if many of those who have that fear realise one or two things with reference to its cause. One

is the appalling speed which the air has brought into
modern warfare. The speed of air attack, compared with
the attack of an army, is as the speed of a motor car to
that of a four-in-hand and in the next war you will find
that any town which is within reach of an aerodrome
can be bombed within the first five minutes of war from
the air, to an extent which was inconceivable in the last
war, and the question will be whose morale will be shattered quickest by that preliminary bombing? I think it is
well for the man in the street to realise that there is no
power on earth that can protect him from being bombed.
Whatever people may tell him, the bomber will always
get through, and it is very easy to understand that if you
realise the area of space ... The only defence is offence,
which means that you have to kill more women and children more quickly than the enemy if you want to save
yourselves.

He went on to talk about the experiments in protection
which had been taking place in continental Europe, especially in relation to gas bombs – this despite the Geneva Gas
Protocol, forbidding the use of gas warfare, which had been
signed by twenty-eight countries in June 1925 and ratified
by Britain in 1929. This, he suggested, was another source
of fear. 'What more potent cause of fear can there be?' he
asked.

And fear is a very dangerous thing. It is quite true that
it can act as a deterrent in people's minds against war,
but it is much more likely to act to make them want to
increase armaments to protect them against the terrors
that they know may be launched against them ... The

prohibition of the bombardment of the civil population ... is impracticable so long as any bombing exists
at all ... We all remember the cry that was raised when
gas was first used, and it was not long before we used
it. We remember also the cry that was raised when civilian towns were first bombed. It was not long before we
replied, and naturally. No one regretted seeing it done
more than I did. It was an extraordinary instance of the
psychological change that comes over all of us in times
of war.

No doubt there were good intentions behind this speech,
but the newspapers seized on one phrase in particular, and
used it to intensify the fears that Baldwin might have been
hoping to allay. 'The bomber will always get through' and
'The only defence is offence' became mantras for the rest of
the decade, used by everyone from the upper echelons of
the RAF to the most sensational thrillers and the most local
organs of the press. And whether the intention was to win
support for rearmament or to raise political consciousness
of the links between capitalism and war, the psychological
result was much the same. Almost a year later, for example,
the first issue of the *Hornsey Rise Estate Express*, a halfpenny
duplicated newspaper put out by local left-wing activists,
led with a front-page story on the Hendon Air Pageant. 'It
will be a fine show ... Probably they will throw in a raid
on a Chinese Village as a special treat at the end.' (One of
the popular spectacles at these shows each year was a
display of RAF planes bombing 'native' villages. In March
1932 the Japanese air force had bombed Shanghai, killing
several thousand civilians. Since then the Japanese had been
bombing and occupying much of northern China. The ironic

implication is therefore quite acute.) The article concluded by quoting Baldwin as a warning: '"The only defence is offence. Which means that you have got to kill more women and children more quickly than the enemy if you want to save yourself." This is the ugly reality behind the stunts and fireworks.'

By 1938 the worst excesses of the imagined apocalypse were being banished. The task by that point, in order to make realistic preparations, was to make the approaching war seem plausible rather than cataclysmic, so many of the central themes of the war literature of the previous fifteen years were restated and reassessed. But they were generally the same themes. Basil Liddell Hart edited a series of eight books under the general title of The Next War. It included volumes on *Gas and Civilians* as well as one on *Air Power*. Sidney Rogerson, writing on propaganda, highlighted the importance of civilian morale, given the 'general recognition' that 'ruthless air raids on open cities, particularly capital cities as the nerve centres of the State, and the terrorisation of their inhabitants by bomb-dealt massacre' would be the 'outstanding feature' of a future European conflict. Propaganda will be important, he argues, because of a 'new and terrifying thing' – the vulnerability of British homes and densely populated towns and cities to war. Morale is what concerns him most, and thinking about its potential breakdown allows him the greatest scope to explore the fears he portrays. His book, like the others in the series, is fundamentally sensible, calling for concerted and serious preparation for a war he regards as inevitable. He is aware of the damage that air raids can do: in his insistence that the population should be defended against 'the fury from the skies' he adduces the example of 'the martyrdom of China' under Japanese bombing. But he wants to see concrete measures taken: he is impatient with the state's reliance on the 'British spirit' – a spirit he describes as 'confused'. One of the primary reasons for this confusion is an influx of 'unstable immigrants, whether from Europe or from Ireland'. 'One has only to remember,' he goes on, 'the disgraceful scenes in East London during air raids in 1917 to realise what a danger these elements can be in spreading hysteria among the more stable indigenous population.' Twenty years later the impact of bombing on morale, so central to the bombers' strategy, is still seen in racial terms. The steady, phlegmatic British may be infected by weak, hysterical foreigners. It is hard to overemphasise the pervasiveness of this sense of Englishness, which constantly reappears in a variety of forms and guises. Even government propaganda was thought of as vaguely foreign and probably a bad thing, so got done amateurishly, without central coordination. The result – castigated by Rogerson – was a series of vague warnings about democracy and 'unfortunately a far greater appeal to fear; fear of bombs, fear of gas, fear of Germany, fear of the future'.

It wouldn't have been so necessary to worry about such fears, however, if they hadn't been the culmination of a decade and a half of powerful fantasy in the wake of the First World War. Almost as popular as the crossword puzzle and the detective story, there was a proliferation of newspaper stories, articles, novels, pamphlets, tracts and books of military, political and technological theory dealing in one way or another with the new threat of war from the air, sometimes coupled with the new threat of Bolshevik revolution.

AIR PERIL

In *The Shape of Things to Come*, H. G. Wells's 1933 'history of the future', which purports to have been written in 2106, someone mentions a retrospective anthology of political comment called *The Sense of Catastrophe in the Nineteen Thirties*. It would not be difficult to compile a book like that. It was clear to many, especially after the Wall Street Crash of 1929, that the whole economic and political system was in crisis; that the 'old gang' of rulers and politicians were unable to solve the problems they'd caused, or were making them worse; and that there was no consensus on an alternative. 'Before the end of the thirties it was plain to all the world that a world-wide social catastrophe was now inevitably in progress,' wrote Wells. When Baldwin made his speech in Parliament in November 1932, the gap between science fiction and scientific prediction narrowed irretrievably. What, until then, had only the powerful but still speculative force of imagination, or the special pleading of military enthusiasts, behind it now seemed, in the context of the current Geneva disarmament talks and with a former prime minister's authority, to have become cold fact. A new flood of books and articles followed, in which fiction and reportage became almost interchangeable. *Invasion from the Air* by Frank McIlraith and Roy Connolly (1934), subtitled 'a prophetic novel', was prefaced by extracts from Baldwin's speech and by a foreword (or 'argument') in which the authors set out the non-fiction basis of their imagined scenario.

> Our novel is based on the theory, supported by a growing body of military opinion, that the decision in the next war will be reached in the air. It has also been accepted that

9. These four dust jackets depict four different styles of representing future air bombardment. The most traditional, Menace, *uses the analogy with an eagle; C. R. W. Nevinson's allegorical painting (which partly inspired the novel) emphasises the vast and monstrous nature of the threat; the design for* Invasion from the Air *stresses the threat to democracy, and recalls the searchlights of the First World War; and Macleish's post-Guernica radio play has a purely stylised image of bombers.*

there is no adequate defence against aerial attack sup-
plemented with gas and fire ... The first result of an air
offensive on a city like London will be the demoralisation of the population, especially when it finds that there
is practically no protection from the deadly gases which
are now carried by bombing aircraft. This demoralisation
will show itself in two ways: (1) in disorder and rioting in
the poor and industrial quarters; (2) by the evacuation of
the higher class residential quarters.

They go on to say that 'a well-informed article in the Daily
Telegraph of November 7th 1933' had envisaged that 80 per
cent of London's population would leave the city within a
week, and that the police would be unable to cope with the
accompanying crime and looting. But the fact that McIlraith
and Connolly chose to write the book in the form of a novel
points up another curious feature of this fascination with
catastrophe: the way that fact and fiction were necessarily
intertwined.

Even at a time when the passion for reportage, documentary film and writing was creating new forms and dis-
seminating new outlooks on the world, there could be no
adequate documentation of the future. However carefully
predictions were presented, and however incontrovertible
they appeared, they had to remain in the realm of imagination, expectation, hope and fear. But there was always a basis
in fact, and the number of facts was always continuing to
increase. In order to make sense of the feeling of conviction in
novels like this, we need to unravel some of the intertwining
strands that made up the apocalyptic vision of the early to
mid-1930s. These will include the development of bombing
as both technology and strategy, concomitant national and

international political arguments, cultural manifestations of air-mindedness – positive and negative – and the emergence of changed literary genres and forms to deal with the new phenomenon.

Since the great increase in the speed of technological change in the nineteenth century, attitudes to machines had become profoundly ambivalent. The aeroplane was the most concise expression so far of this ambivalence. Flight, so long the dream of earthbound humans, became perhaps the most important and most contested symbol of power and freedom. Bombing, which flight made possible, embodied perhaps the most atavistic fear: the fear that the sky might any day fall on one's head. The fear of science and technology was further focused in the fear of airborne chemical warfare, with its threat of choking, paralysing or fatal gas, and of biological warfare, spreading incurable and dreadful disease. Naturally these ambivalent attitudes to the discoveries of science and the uses to which they might be put were further shaped by the vast complex of conflicting political, moral and symbolic ideas which animated the early twentieth century.

The last decade of the nineteenth century had seen a millennial explosion in writing about the future. Social, medical and technological progress, feminism, eugenics and socialism provoked a huge range of predictive books and articles. To some it must have seemed as if Utopia was within reach. But even in Utopia the prospect of a cataclysm was never far away, either cleansing, destroying or providing yet another new opportunity, as in H. G. Wells' opportunistic idea of a 'war that will end war' with which he greeted the coming of the First World War in 1914. Early fantasies about air power, such as Stanley Waterloo's *Armageddon* (1898), presented the aeroplane as a romantically conceived guarantor of national independence, a heroic expression of English, French, German or American superiority. They encapsulated what was standard military doctrine at the end of the nineteenth century and became a central strand of strategic thinking between the First and Second World Wars: that the more technologically sophisticated war became, the sooner wars would be concluded and therefore the more civilised they would become. I. F. Clarke effectively describes the 'compound of complacency, ignorance, and innocence' which animated so many of the war and future-war stories of the period and contributed largely to British attitudes at the start of the First World War.

It was Wells again who was one of the first to imagine and describe a less reassuring side of scientific progress: the 'air menace' as it would soon be known, in his 1908 novel *War in the Air*. In this, Germany, 'by far the most efficient power in the world, better organised for swift and secret action, better equipped with the resources of modern science', has developed new weapons and is therefore poised to seize control of the air, to 'strike and conquer – before the others had anything but experiments in the air'. The use of bombs is fairly marginal, but the ultimate consequence of a rapid spiral of scientific inventions in the service of a world war is the destruction of civilisation itself. The narrative becomes increasingly apocalyptic, drawing on the already existing novelistic convention of some cataclysm returning nations to a primitive or pre-scientific age; visions of progress and uncertainties about modernisation, sometimes coupled with an alarmed social Darwinism, produced a spate of late-nineteenth century novels of pessimistic or optimistic destruction. Novels like Richard Jefferies's *After London*

(1885) or W. H. Hudson's *A Crystal Age* (1887) suggested a different, more Arcadian, approach to contemporary problems; others warned of the dangers of science by stressing the need to keep control of potent discoveries in the right (usually British) hands.

As early as April 1914 Colonel Louis Jackson warned of the consequences of a 'knock-out blow' from the air. 'Panic and riot' might follow, and the destruction of civilian morale might force the government to 'accept an unfavourable peace'. Although villagers in the Middle East had been subjected to bombing raids before 1915, it was the people of London and Paris who were the first in Europe to experience the horror of being bombed from the air. In fact two small bombs were dropped on the outskirts of Paris by a German pilot as early as 14 August 1914. Rear Admiral Behnke, deputy chief of the German Naval Command, was convinced that dropping bombs on London and its docks could 'cause panic in the population' to such an extent that war could not continue. At the start of the war, British planes dropped bombs on the German Zeppelin sheds in an unsuccessful attempt to prevent such German raids; nevertheless there were a number of raids by Zeppelins in 1915 and 1916, though the cumbersome and poorly equipped airships often lost their way in the blackout and were forced to choose targets other than their intended ones. Possibly as few as 10 per cent of the bombs found their proper targets, which contributed to the sense of outrage when bombs fell on houses, schools and hospitals. Hull suffered two major raids, and Tyneside – especially Hartlepool – was also hit. In all, the Zeppelins dropped about 6,000 bombs, killing 556 and wounding 1,357. But their symbolic effect was a more powerful one. Looking back on 1915 in his novel *Kangaroo*

10. *The first bombs were grenades or hand-held explosive devices, their accuracy dependent on the eye and arm of the bomber. It seems almost like cricket as this Sidney Riesenberg illustration of an airman bombing a Zeppelin very clearly shows.*

(1923), D. H. Lawrence remembered 'the war horror drifting in, drifting in, prices rising, excitement growing, people
going mad about the Zeppelin raids'. It was the moment
the old world ended. 'In the winter of 1915–1916 … the city
in some way perished, perished from being a heart of the
world, and became a vortex of broken passions, lusts, hopes,
fears, and horrors.' The bombs were not solely responsible
for this sense of an ending, of the fall of a civilisation, but
they were its most dramatic manifestation.

ZEPPELIN NIGHTS

The first of the Zeppelin raids over London, on 31 May 1915,
killed seven civilians and injured thirty-five. This did not
result in the kind of demoralised panic the Germans had
hoped for, but it certainly frightened people. The poet Iris
Tree vividly evokes the feeling in the opening lines of her
1915 poem 'Zeppelins':

> Suddenly
> Shutting our lips upon a jest
> As we are sipping thoughts from little glasses
> A gun bursts thunder and the echoing streets
> Quiver with startled terrors—
> How swift runs fear …

The airships usually flew too high for the anti-aircraft
guns, and if they were hit the inadequate ammunition
seldom penetrated their casing. This changed in 1916, when
the Royal Flying Corps was issued with incendiary bullets
that could explode a Zeppelin in mid-air. By the end of that
year the airships had been largely phased out, replaced by

Gotha and Giant aeroplanes capable of speeds of seventy to eighty-five miles per hour, which were much faster, and more difficult to deal with. When the Germans bombed Folkestone in May 1917 (killing 95 and injuring 195), the 74 British fighters which tried to engage the group of bombers managed to shoot down only one of the enemy planes. The worst of these air raids happened on 13 June 1917, when 128 bombs were dropped from a fleet of 14 planes, killing as many as 162 people and injuring 432. It was a daylight raid on an almost cloudless day, particularly memorable for one episode. Bombs fell on the LCC school in Upper North Street, Poplar (near the London docks), killing eighteen children, all but two of them aged six and under, and injuring thirty-four. The joint funeral – decribed as 'one of the most impressive ever seen in the East End of London' – made an indelible impression, and was one of the factors responsible for the decision to evacuate children from the East End in the Second World War. Two more typical Gotha raids were on 17 February 1918, when twenty were killed and twenty-two injured at St Pancras station, and on 7 March, when a 1,000-kg bomb demolished four houses in Paddington, with ten more severely damaged and another four hundred suffering some degree of damage. The last raid of the war occurred on 19 May 1918.

When the Zeppelin raids started, some people in London sought shelter in Underground stations, and when the more serious Gotha and Giant raids began at the end of 1917 they moved in in large numbers. In early 1918 up to 300,000 Londoners were regularly using the Tube stations as shelters, encouraged by the Underground railway companies, who even took advantage of the raids to advertise 'It is bomb proof down below.' The government was not very happy about the use of the Tube, especially at first, prefer-ring people to stay in their homes or in neighbouring cellars. 'It is generally desirable,' said the Home Secretary, trying to keep things tidy, 'that people should be encouraged to stay in their own homes.' A leaflet put out by the Hampstead Council of Social Welfare argued that 'the diseases caused by crowding in the Tubes, the weariness, sleepiness and excite-ment of little children, are a greater danger to life than all the guns put together. The London hospitals scarcely felt the air raid casualties; it was the children's hospitals afterwards that had the work to do.' Basil Liddell Hart made a similar point in *Paris; or the Future of War* in 1925: 'Who that saw it will ever forget the nightly sight of the population of a great industrial and shipping town, such as Hull, streaming out into the fields on the first sound of the alarm signals? Women, children, babies in arms, spending night after night huddled in sodden fields, shivering under a bitter wintry sky – the exposure must have caused far more harm than the few bombs dropped from two or three Zeppelins.' There was probably more concern expressed over the moral and psy-chological effects of bombing than for the material destruc-tion wrought by the bombs themselves (some thirty tonnes of bombs were dropped on London overall, causing 1,880 casualties; nationally, just over 1,400 people died from air raids, and 3,416 were injured). Even so, defence of the capital was a major undertaking: by 1918 the air defence of London consisted of a force of 414 aeroplanes, 480 anti-aircraft guns, 700 searchlights and 15,000 men.

The anxiety about the moral and psychological effects of bombing was not unfounded. Zeppelins could and did cause panic, and steps had to be taken to control people's behav-iour to prevent fear spreading like contagion among the

11. *This crude First World War poster shows a Zeppelin caught in the beam of a searchlight. More interestingly, it exploits the idea that bombs are for civilians, and that men of fighting age ought to be facing bullets rather than meeting a death that is somehow less manly because not met at the front.*

crowds, as psychologists believed it would. The need people felt to keep their wilder emotions under control can be seen in some of the literature of the time. F. S. Flint's impressionist poem 'Zeppelins' gives a vivid glimpse of this:

> From a blur of female faces
> Distraught eyes stand out,
> And a woman's voice cries:
> 'The Zeppelins – they are attacking us;
> [...] I shiver: chill? excitement? fear?

and Laurence Binyon's 'The Zeppelin', with its similar evocation of alarm and unlit streets, tries patriotically, and propagandistically, to convert fear into indignation:

> Guns! far and near.
> Quick, sudden, angry,
> They startle the still street.
> Upturned faces appear,
> Doors open on darkness,
> There is hurrying of feet.
> . . . .
> Is it terror you seek
> To exult in? Know then
> Hearts are here
> That the plunging beak
> Of night-winged havoc
> Strikes not with fear
>
> So much as it strings
> To a deep elation
> And a quivering pride
> That at last the hour brings
> For them too the danger
> Of those who died. …

The expectation of panic could be mocked, too. In Stephen Phillips's 1915 play *Armageddon*, a German reporter absurdly regales an official of the German Press Bureau with the stories he wants to hear about London:

> The panic in London which broke out on the declaration of war with Germany shows no sign of abatement. Business

has been for some time at a standstill ... Not a sound is to be heard but from time to time the sullen and terrifying drone of our aeroplanes, or still more awful spectacle of a Zeppelin, too high up to be scrutinised. Occasionally you may see the white faces of scared tradesmen start up for a moment from various cellars, where the majority of Londoners now spend the long nights in a fever of apprehension.

Not that comedy always needed to be fabricated: after the first Zeppelin raid, the headline in the *Daily News* for 1 June 1915 reassuringly read, 'ZEPPELIN RAID OVER OUTER LONDON, Many Fires reported but These not Absolutely Connected with Airships.' The same unsnappy way with words was to be seen in a British propaganda poster from the same year. In lurid colour, it depicted a woman and child being blown up by a bomb dropped from a Zeppelin. Its message was 'Enlist. By staying at home you are giving your approval to this sort of thing.' But perhaps the most elegant and interesting writing inspired by the Zeppelin raids was *Zeppelin Nights*, by Violet Hunt and Ford Madox Hueffer, a powerful and entertaining update of Boccaccio's *Decameron*, in which a group of people dispel their fear of the raids by telling stories, which themselves gradually provide a moral and intellectual background to the war: 'We could see the sky, fairly clear, white without being light, seared and blanched by the eager searchlights. The shafts pried, peered, pierced the beguiling clouds that might have held, somewhere in their dovelike folds, the approaching doom of London.' In another gesture of support for social cohesion, the main character (who is actually forty) gives a false age and joins the army, arguing that poets have no more right to avoid the fighting than members of any other trade or profession. So much for the destruction of morale. As Tami Davis Biddle has shown, 'the British were angry and indignant about the poor state of their defences, and outraged that their government seemed so inept ... but there is no evidence of persistent, widespread, or deep-seated panic over the Zeppelin raids.' Whatever individual responses may have been, the collective response was not at all what Behnke had predicted.

In *Finding Time Again*, the final volume of Proust's novel *In Search of Lost Time*, Marcel and Saint-Loup watch a Zeppelin raid on Paris, picking out the beauty of the defending aeroplanes in their star-like formations, and the 'Wagnerian' sirens. The ceaselessly questing searchlights – so often described or evoked in poems and paintings during the war – and the 'shattering sound of the sirens' create what Proust calls 'an apocalypse in the sky', with a comic farce of frightened figures scuttling about in their nightwear at ground level providing a counterpart to the sublime drama played out in the heavens above. It does not seem to be able to inspire fear in him, though – not until a few days later, when he is caught in another air raid and catches sight of a pilot in the act of dropping a bomb.

> Isolated thoughts about bombs being thrown, or about the possibility of death, added nothing tragic to the image I had formed of the passing German airships, until, from one of them, buffeted by winds and partly hidden from my gaze by the billowing mists of a troubled sky, from an aeroplane which, even though I knew it was murderous, I still imagined only to be stellar and heavenly, I had seen, one evening, the gesture of a bomb dropped down

towards us. For the true reality of a danger is perceived only in that new thing, irreducible to what one already knows, which we call an impression.

For most, that impression was linked more with the effects of the bombs than with the act of dropping them.

'FRIGHTFULNESS'

At the first Hague peace conference of 1899, a principle that had been enshrined in warfare since the Middle Ages, that only fortified towns might be attacked, was abandoned, and other targets were made legitimate objects of attack. In 1907, at the second conference, attended by forty-six nations rather than the twenty-six that sent delegates to the first, the bombardment from the sea of undefended towns was recognised as a permitted act of war. Illogically perhaps, even very small attacks in which modified grenades were dropped from the air were not. The air seemed still to be an impassable frontier. In principle these conferences (which had been jointly called by Tsar Nicholas II and Queen Wilhelmina of the Netherlands) were designed to encourage disarmament, and so were prepared to put restrictions on the newest form of warfare. But permitted or not (and ratification of resolutions is always a problem), the first aerial attacks were carried out by the Italians during their war with Turkey in 1911. On 1 November that year a Lieutenant Cavotti of the Italian Air Fleet dropped four 2-kg bombs on Turkish positions in Tripoli, and in the following days several more were dropped on nearby Arab bases. Some apparently fell on a field hospital, at Ain Zara – the first in a long series of similar assaults on humanitarian conventions which continues to provoke controversy over bombing almost a hundred years later. This first incident provoked argument in the press of a number of countries – not only the combatants' – about the ethics of dropping bombs from the air. The Italians were very struck by the 'wonderful moral effect' of bombing (by which they meant the effect on morale). In this they were confirming Major Robert Baden-Powell's pronouncement two years earlier, that airships would be a great asset in 'savage warfare' because 'the moral effect on an ignorant enemy would be great, and a few bombs would cause serious panics'. This belief was to dominate thinking about air warfare for the next twenty years.

During the First World War, bombing technology advanced significantly. There were neither bomb racks nor bombsights in 1914; by the end of the war, custom-designed heavy bombers – the Handley Page, the Gotha – were in production, with larger planes like the Vickers Vimy approaching readiness. In the wake of the war, with the advent of the new threat of aerial bombardment, and the potentially limitless scope of attack from the air, many people felt there was an urgent need to institute some kind of internationally recognised regulation of bombing. In 1923, Air Warfare Rules were drawn up which restricted aerial bombing to military objectives only, and specifically prohibited 'aerial bombardment for the purpose of terrorising the civilian population, of destroying or damaging private property not of a military character, or of injuring non-combatants'. But the reason why regulation was needed was precisely because these were believed to be the most potent and most effective ways of using bombs. Not only were they envisaged, they were in quite widespread use. The prohibition enshrined in the Rules can be seen paradoxically as indicating a general recognition of this, even as a sort of elegy for a time when the practice of war could be confined to unpopulated battlefields (if such a time ever existed). By making bombing of civilians the subject of explicit regulation it also increased public fears.

One of the earliest enthusiasts for bombing was Winston Churchill. In 1912, when he was First Lord of the Admiralty, he had encouraged the navy to start experimenting with bombs. At the start of the First World War he was asked, as Secretary of State for the Admiralty, to take responsibility for the aerial defence of Britain, and he energetically set about creating a system of searchlights and anti-aircraft guns. But he recognised that the only effective defence would be from aircraft themselves, to prevent the bombers from getting through. When, as Minister of Munitions in October 1917, he wrote a memorandum in which he outlined the likely future of air power in war, he was cautious about the idea of an air offensive, and sceptical of the 'knock-out blow', arguing that it was

not reasonable to speak of an air offensive as if it were going to finish the war by itself. It is improbable that any terrorisation of the civil population which could be achieved by air attack would compel the government of a great nation to surrender. Familiarity with bombardment, a good system of dug-outs or shelters, a strong control by police and military authorities, should be sufficient to preserve the national fighting power unimpaired. In our own case we have seen the combative spirit of the people roused, and not quelled, by the German air raids. Nothing that we have learned of the capacity of the German population to endure suffering justifies us in assuming that they could be cowed into submission by such methods, or, indeed, that they would not be rendered more desperately resolved by them.

He therefore argued against attacking civilian or indiscriminate targets, advocating instead attacks on the enemy's bases and communications.

Churchill's memo was responding to a report for the British government in which General Smuts recommended the establishment of an Air Ministry to coordinate the different sections of air warfare, including an Independent Air Force to carry out long range strategic bombing missions. 'The day may not be far off when aerial operations with their devastation of enemy lands and destruction of industrial and populous centres on a vast scale may become the principal operations of war,' Smuts wrote. It rapidly became an article of faith in the War Office and the newly formed RAF that huge bombing raids on enemy cities would utterly destroy a nation's will to resist. Where Churchill saw a difference between war and the political control of inferior races or classes, supporters of offensive bombing regarded all populations as subject to the same demoralising fear.

One powerful reason for this was Britain's colonial experience. The history of bombing policy in Britain between the wars is deeply involved with the RAF's quest for independence from the other two arms of the military, and with the history of interwar British colonialism. The most crucial distinction here is between citizens of Britain and Europe and colonial subjects overseas. In 1920, when the threat of revolution prompted the government to pass the Emergency Powers Act, Chief of the Air Staff Sir Hugh Trenchard wrote a draft paper for Churchill on ways in which the air force

12. *British aircraft bomb the Afghan capital of Kabul on 17 May 1919, in a fanciful illustration by Achille Beltrame for the Italian publication* La Domenica del Corriere.

might be used to quell revolt. His most alarming suggestion was that if situations arose, as he thought they might, in which English cities became hostile to the government, 'a limited amount of bombing' by the RAF might be sanctioned.

Churchill, horrified, if not by the idea, at least by the thought that it might get into the press, insisted on all references to England and Ireland being removed, and on the paper being generally toned down. In fact armed aeroplanes *were* in service against the republicans in Ireland in 1921, but no bombs were dropped. Nevertheless, the state had considered using bombs against its own citizens.

There were fewer scruples with what was euphemistically known as 'imperial defence'. Bombs were being used against tribesmen on the Indian frontier from 1915 onward, and they were also used in Darfur in 1916 and in Somaliland. Driving the 'Mad Mullah' out of Somaliland in the winter of 1919–20 was presented as a perfect example of how air control could work. The fear of being bombed was more powerful even than troublesome native belief systems. 'No magic survives a good bombing,' wrote Sir John Slessor, then a flight commander in India, with evident satisfaction. With the post-First World War peace settlement and the expropriation of the Turks, the imperial 'civilising mission' was extended, but not always or everywhere welcomed. As George Orwell put it twenty years later, 'Defenceless villages are bombarded from the air, the inhabitants driven out into the countryside, the cattle machine-gunned, the huts set on fire with incendiary bullets: this is called *pacification*.' And the military vocabulary that Orwell mocks is indeed very revealing. The single word which stood in for all the consequences of bombing and shooting civilians – blowing them up, maiming, wounding, disfiguring or bereaving them, killing their animals, and destroying their homes and livelihoods – was 'frightfulness'. This is the word that crops up all the time in official discussions of policy. And, while the blandness and distaste for real thought it represents are almost palpable, it became a potent term in the argument against bombing in the 1920s. The most widely read attack on the official policy, *The Great Delusion* (1927), by 'Neon' (Marion Acworth), denounced the idea that the British should simply 'take frightfulness as a matter of course'. Was there any moral difference, the author asked, 'between the killing of British women and children by the bombing of London and the recent bombing of totally defenceless women and children [by the RAF] in their native villages in Waziristan?' But in the end the word was used so much that it lost any residual sense of horror that it may once have had and became just another technical term, as in this 1938 comment: 'A further development of aerial frightfulness recently perfected in Spain and China is the machine gunning of civilians from the air.'

This impersonal use of language was central to the need that military strategists and some politicians felt to distance themselves from the moral consequences of their policies. Ways had to be found of policing the Empire without bankrupting the armed forces, and the air force seemed to offer the best answers. Not only could it cover more ground more quickly than infantry, regardless of the terrain (as long as it wasn't mountainous or heavily forested – deserts were best), but its real effectiveness was believed to be moral: the fear induced by single acts of violent destruction would, they were confident, have long term intimidatory effects. It was not usually couched in clear terms, though. The public perception of this exemplary violence had to remain politically acceptable. Indeed the very 'impersonality' of air operations (or their 'inhumanity', depending on one's point of view) made them more vulnerable to criticism than the army, which for example used gas shells extensively in 1920 in what is now Iraq. (Many prominent figures supported the use of gas; Churchill was 'strongly in favour of using poisoned gas against uncivilised tribes', and T. E. Lawrence wrote to *The Observer* newspaper in 1920 to say that he thought it was 'odd we do not use poison gas' against rebellious tribesmen.) The RAF by contrast was not allowed to use them. Those in control of the RAF, like Trenchard, were convinced that morale was the key to submission, and submission the guarantee of peace. Those on the ground who had to live with the consequences were not so sure.

By the early 1930s the air-force hegemony was weakening; air control was reduced in the fight against Waziristan rebels in India in 1931. Field Marshal Sir Philip Chetwode, the commander-in-chief in India, told the viceroy of India, 'I loathe bombing, and never agree to it without a guilty conscience.' It was, he went on, 'a revolting method of making war, especially by a great power against tribesmen'. In the same year the government briefly considered bombing the ships occupied in Scotland by the Invergordon mutineers, but decided against it. The Cabinet's apprehension about the counterproductive consequences of bombing civilians was evidenced again in the summer of 1936, during the Palestinian Revolt. Air Vice-Marshal Peirse, air officer commanding British forces in Palestine, wanted to use bombers to wipe out villages and to bomb Nablus in order to 'cow the country'. The Cabinet disagreed, and removed Peirse from his command, replacing him with an army lieutenant-general.

Writing of the abhorrence with which most people outside the air force regarded the 'clinical professionalism' of the RAF, Charles Townshend says, 'There was an idea that air attack was in some sense wrong, in a way that traditional forms of land and sea attack were not. Against this irrational instinct the RAF battled persistently, and with little reward.' This is not very surprising, since what the RAF saw as mechanistic or logistical problems everybody else saw as an extension of the savage mechanisation of war that had resulted in the slaughter of 1914–18. Even more important perhaps than the mechanistic problems was the powerful sense that air attack was in a profound way unfair, whether the target was 'underdeveloped' tribespeople or civilians in Europe. And it might be used against us if we used it against others. In 1922 the military theorist J. F. C. Fuller had argued that air power was unsuitable for 'pacification' as it could cause only 'obliteration'. While it could persuade peoples to accept British rule, it was incapable, others argued, of instilling respect for the central principles of the Empire, 'integrity, justice and humanity'. Speaking in the House of Lords in 1930, Lord Lloyd put his finger on what was the most salient feature of all: control from the air was 'an impersonal and inhuman agency'. This reflected the focus of people's fear: that death from the air was outside the boundaries within which normal life, and even life in wartime, was carried on; it escaped the social and stimulated a more intense notion of vulnerability, and of the random nature of mortality. This disagreement about the RAF's attitude structured the arguments about 'frightfulness' which lasted from 1920 until the area bombings of the Second World War, and beyond.

To many people, the RAF appeared to embody a new way of thinking – one that was detached, inhuman and strangely removed from the claims of sympathy or morality; one that had discarded the defining British ethic of 'fair play'. Sentimentalism had no place in the world of total war. When W. H. Auden wrote in a 1930 poem of 'the hawk' and 'the helmeted airman', the implied comparison is very clear. Both in appearance (the dehumanising helmet and goggles) and action (the sudden rapacious kill from above) the airman is different from the rest of us. The bird's-eye view can be presented as clear-sighted, offering the kind of impartial, perspectival and historically informed overview needed by democracies. The airman can dramatise the new scientific vision. But in some treatments he can also exploit it to appear as a new man, an *Übermensch*, untroubled by Victorian or Christian notions of morality, a powerful leader who will establish a new sense of social purpose. This figure has obvious parallels with fascist ideologies, and it may draw on other characteristics of the hawk, like predation, savagery and speed. The corollary was a comment by one of the leaders of the disarmament movement, the Revd Canon Charles Raven, who claimed in 1936 that it was 'utterly inconceivable that Christ could be the pilot of a bombing aeroplane'.

One of the most powerful commentaries on all this is to be found in Bertrand Russell's 1938 essay *Power*. He cites an account, by Mussolini's son Bruno, of the pleasure of bombing Abyssinians: 'We had to set fire to wooded hills, to the fields and little villages ... It was all most diverting ... After the bomb-racks were emptied I began throwing bombs by hand ... I had to aim carefully at the straw roof and only succeeded at the third shot. The wretches who were inside, seeing their roof burning, jumped out and ran off like mad. Surrounded by a circle of fire about five thousand Abyssinians came to a sticky end.' Men who can act and think like this, Russell comments, men 'whose love of power has been fed by control over mechanism', or even a union of scientific technologists, might in the future establish an oligarchy in which the consent of the governed is unnecessary, and where control could be established through the use of technology, poison gas, or bacteria. The men in control 'would view human material as they had learnt to view their own machines'. Having pondered the consequences of a separation between power and people such as comes from living in high towers or in aeroplanes, and concluding that a government of such rulers would have little profound concern for the happiness of its subjects and less compunction about exterminating resistance, Russell concludes that machines create a new mentality. 'The man who has vast mechanical power at his command is likely, if uncontrolled, to feel himself a god – not a Christian God of Love, but a pagan Thor or Vulcan.' The airman, or the type he symbolises, becomes an unfeeling consciousness, intrinsically antisocial, his plane a great metal prosthesis.

How does this relate to the central claim that the effect of bombing was moral rather than merely destructive? The use of air-policing methods in the inhospitable terrain of the Middle East and Sudan was partly attractive to government because it was much cheaper and more cost-effective than the use of land troops and the long lines of support and communication they required. The moral argument rested on the powers of destruction that aircraft could command, and on ideas about the primitive mentality of those who were bombed. When it was suggested that 'the psychology of the tribesman' was not all that different from that of the average British citizen, the RAF reply was scornful: 'It is of course fantastic to suggest that the psychology of the tribesmen, who spend half their lives shooting at each other, is similar to that of an English villager.' Colonial administrators were not well disposed towards rebels, or even those who were acquiescent in British rule, but the literal detachment of the air force seemed to set them at an even greater distance: from the RAF's bird's-eye viewpoint, a ruthless campaign that bullied people into submission was the most effective means of colonial rule.

According to David Omissi, the 'moral effect' of bombing shifted around 1924 from the imposition of heavy casualties to 'the indefinite disruption of everyday life'. And bombing raids were increasingly preceded by some kind of warning, to minimise human casualties. Casualties were still caused indirectly, however – by bombing irrigation systems, dispersing or destroying livestock, destroying field terraces, burning crops. But in the five years before that, hundreds if not thousands of tribespeople had been killed by bombing in Sudan, Afghanistan, Iraq and the North West Frontier. The bodily mutilation caused by the bombs was regarded by some airmen as a bonus, as it made the threat of raids even more frightening to the villagers. Omissi illustrates this attitude with chilling effect, citing Squadron Leader Arthur (later 'Bomber') Harris in 1924: 'The Arab and Kurd ... now know what real bombing means, in casualty and damage; they now know that within 45 minutes a full sized village can be practically wiped out and a third of its inhabitants killed or injured by four or five machines, which offer them no real target, no opportunity for glory as warriors, no effective means of escape.'

It was not until the 1930s that colonial policymakers recognised that the bombing caused too much uncontrollable damage to be an effective part of the apparatus of policing and control, and even then they continued to use it where they deemed it necessary, as in the Yemen and Palestine. This was accompanied by growing claims (which have a decidedly familiar ring today) for the precision and accuracy of bombing, and the ability of the air force to target houses of hostile individuals and leave others untouched. Such propaganda claims were almost entirely false, and known to be so: well over 50 per cent of bombs missed their target villages completely, and surgical precision was well beyond the capability of any ordinary bombing mission between the wars.

TREMENDOUS – BUT *WRONG*

This change of attitude was partly associated with the shifting public opinion of bombing in the light of discussions at the Geneva Disarmament Conference, which opened in 1932. (It was a debate on the conference that gave Baldwin the opportunity to make his famous speech.) Serious and numerous attempts were being made there to ban the use of the bomber in war. This appeared to be a much less utopian demand than it now looks: at several points the conference apparently came near to achieving agreement. In March 1933, Part II, Section II, Chapter 3, Article 34 of the text adopted in the First Reading of the Draft Convention for the Reduction and Limitation of Armaments stated, 'The High Contracting Parties accept the complete abolition of bombing from the air (except for police purposes in outlying regions).' Only the Japanese delegation completely rejected the prohibition of bombing. Germany and others even proposed prohibiting preparations for bombing, too, and some countries, including the United States, wanted to extend the prohibition completely and not exclude the 'outlying regions'. In fact, however, the influence of the RAF was decisive. One of the reasons a final agreement was not reached was the British refusal to agree to stop using bombs for the purposes of colonial 'pacification' in those 'outlying regions'.

It would be wrong to conclude from this, however, that other countries were not also keen on using bombing as a significant weapon in colonial territories. France, Spain and Italy all used it extensively, as did the Japanese in their war against China. In Cuba, General Machado's planes bombed the town of Gibara to put down a local uprising. France used terror bombing almost continuously in 1925 and 1926 against the Druze rebels in Syria, subjecting the villages around Damascus especially to frequent and unannounced bombardment. The acting British consul in Damascus, quoted by Omissi, thought that the French were pursuing 'a sustained policy of "frightfulness" intended to terrify and exhaust the rebels into absolute submission'. In October 1925 the French even went so far as to bomb the Muslim old-town sections of Damascus itself, destroying mosques and palaces and killing some 1,400 civilians. Far from pacifying the rebels, the result of this policy was, not surprisingly, to intensify hostility to the French. When the Japanese bombed the Chinese district of Shanghai on 28 January 1932, they too intensified Chinese hatred of the invader, inaugurating a campaign that would last until the start of the Second World War and beyond. Once the Sino-Japanese War was officially under way, in 1937, Japanese bombers killed tens of thousands of civilians. A contemporary newspaper report provides a typical account, and quotes the by now routine denial by the perpetrators. Reading it, and remembering Franco's denial of the bombing of Guernica, it's hard not to recall fondly the newspaperman's motto adopted by Claud Cockburn: 'Never believe anything until it has been officially denied.'

The greater part of Shanghai's industrial areas have been to a considerable extent destroyed. Japanese air forces have also inaugurated a systematic bombing of Chinese territory all round the French Concession and International Settlement from close up to the boundaries far into the interior in their alleged attempts to break up Chinese troop concentrations. These air raids have resulted in an enormous loss of civilian life and destruction of property of no military importance whatsoever. Many undefended cities, devoid of all troops, have been mercilessly bombed. One of the most flagrant cases of this massacring of Chinese non-combatants took place on August 18, when Japanese aeroplanes deliberately bombed Shanghai South Station at a time when it was crowded with refugees waiting for a train to take them to Hangchow. About a hundred and seventy people were killed, mostly women and children, and many more wounded. Reputable foreign newspaper correspondents, who had watched the bombing and were on the spot shortly after it took place, aver that there were no Chinese soldiers in evidence and none amongst the killed. Foreign medical men in the hospitals which received the wounded also testify that there were no soldiers amongst them, and that they were mostly women and children. Thus the statement issued by the Japanese military spokesman that those killed and wounded in this bombing were nearly all soldiers must be branded as a pure fabrication, designed to mislead the world as to the real activities of Japanese bombers.

Attacks on Shanghai were particularly heavy, but there were also major bombardments of Canton, Hankow and

Chungking. Railway stations, hospitals and Red Cross units were targeted, and on 26 August two cars carrying Sir Hughe Knatchbull-Hugessen, the British ambassador to China, and his entourage were machine-gunned and bombed on roads outside the war zone. (The ambassador was seriously injured.) But, despite being some of the most extensive and destructive bombardments of the decade, these made only a limited impression in Europe. There were questions in the House of Commons, diplomatic representations through the ambassador in Tokyo, and protests from the mayors of eleven British cities, as well as many towns in other countries, but little was achieved. Geoffrey Mander, a Liberal MP, asked Prime Minister Neville Chamberlain whether the government proposed to do anything 'apart from holding up their hands in horror'. Chamberlain replied that 'If we could ... we certainly would do so.' But it seemed they couldn't. The French and the Americans protested too, but the Japanese responded that they were no more bombing civilians deliberately than Britain had been bombing non-combatants in Waziristan (about which there had recently been a mass protest meeting in Allahabad). This gave rise to what now seems a quite grotesque exchange in the House of Commons on 17 June 1937. Sir Percy Harris asked the Prime Minister whether it wouldn't be a 'splendid gesture to the world' if Britain abandoned the practice of 'police bombing' in India, since it was being used by Franco and the Japanese to justify their attacks on civilians. 'No, I do not think it would be a splendid gesture,' Chamberlain replied, and added that the practice was 'in the main, I think, humane'.

In March 1938 W. H. Auden and Christopher Isherwood watched a Japanese air raid on Hankow. They waited on

*13. This Chinese cartoon by Yet Chian-yu shows how universal the
experience of bombing was. The economic image is reduced to the four basic
elements: bombing planes, a family, fear and flight. This image was used by
Faber & Faber on the dust jacket of Auden and Isherwood's* Journey to a
War, *and as its frontispiece.*

a roof with the British consul and others; the sirens had
sounded for a second time.

> A pause. Then far off, the hollow, approaching roar of the
> bombers, boring their way invisibly through the dark.
> The dull, punching thud of bombs falling, near the air-
> field, out in the suburbs. The searchlights criss-crossed,
> plotting points, like dividers; and suddenly there they
> were, six of them, flying close together and high up. It
> was as if a microscope had brought dramatically into
> focus the bacilli of a fatal disease. They passed, bright,

tiny, and deadly, infecting the night. The searchlights followed them right across the sky: guns smashed out; tracer-bullets bounced up towards them, falling hopelessly short, like slow-motion rockets. The concussions made you catch your breath; the watchers around us on the roof exclaimed softly, breathlessly: 'Look! look! there!' It was as tremendous as Beethoven, but *wrong* – a cosmic offence, an insult to the whole of Nature, and the entire earth. I don't know if I was frightened. Something inside me was flapping about like a fish.

This careful, detailed account contrasts powerfully with the apocalyptic tropes and language of much earlier popular fiction and debate, in which the same key images were repeated time and again. They were derived on the whole from the stock vocabulary of natural disaster, Armageddon, earthquake and apocalypse, with heavy echoes of H. G. Wells and, later, Giulio Douhet (much of whose scenario of disaster was anyway derived from his own enthusiasm for Wells). So in 1923 we find J. F. C. Fuller describing in *The Reformation of War* how

> great cities, such as London, will be attacked from the air … Picture, if you will, what the result will be: London for several days will be one vast raving Bedlam, the hospitals will be stormed, traffic will cease, the homeless will shriek for help, the city will be in pandemonium. What of the government at Westminster? It will be swept away by an avalanche of terror. Then will the enemy dictate his terms … Thus may a war be won in forty-eight hours and the losses of the winning side may actually be nil!

Madness, terror and pandemonium, followed by moral collapse. Fuller's ideas were explicitly referenced in Shaw Desmond's baroque fantasy novel *Ragnarok: A Novel of the Future* (1926), but in the context of a complete (and deserved) collapse of civilisation, rather than an attempt to reform it.

In *Janus or the Conquest of War* (1927) the psychologist William McDougall, all too aware of the human aggressive instinct, wrote:

> The developments of the arts of destruction ... especially the development of aircraft, of the explosive bomb and of the poison gases, have made it only too clear that in the next Great War the civilian populations, and especially the populations of the great cities, will be the first and greatest sufferers, that wounds, mutilation and death, terror and famine, will be broadcast among them with awful impartiality; that no woman, no family, no little child, no church, no treasury of art, no museum of priceless antiquities, no shrine of learning and science will be immune; but that in a few days or hours great cities may be levelled with the dust, while their surviving inhabitants scrape for crusts amid mangled bodies of fair women and the ruins of the monuments of art and science.

This vision of 'impartial' destruction focuses on the products of civilisation – which is all but allegorised in the figure of the 'fair women' and their 'mangled bodies' – in support of McDougall's argument for prevention, rather than cure. He proposes an international air police to 'allay the fear of aggression'. The desire in this passage is clearly to shock, but the terms used are already losing their force.

Another book in the same series as McDougall's was Basil

Liddell Hart's *Paris; or the Future of War* (1925). Liddell Hart asks his reader to 'imagine for a moment London, Manchester, Birmingham, and half a dozen other great centres simultaneously attacked, the business localities and Fleet Street wrecked, Whitehall a heap of ruins, the slum districts maddened into the impulse to break loose and maraud, the railways cut, factories destroyed'. This is a nation demoralised. The trope relies on another much-used figure: the idea of the city as a 'nerve-centre', the centre of 'will and policy'. London, the greatest city in the world, contained the seat of government of both Britain and its empire, the royal family, the Stock Exchange, banks, insurance companies, churches, art galleries, museums, docks and factories. And millions of houses. Yet the great city, seen from above, is presented as an image of vulnerability. 'A nation's nerve-system no longer covered by the flesh of its troops, is now laid bare to attack,' flayed and vulnerable as an anatomical illustration in a medical textbook. If you deranged the nerve-centre 'would not the general will to resist vanish?' Civilisation requires control, including control of the lower classes: ordinary social anxieties are intensified by these visions of war. This control is the new 'moral objective' introduced by air warfare, and the idea that fear leads to madness, and madness to uncontrolled 'marauding' and chaos, is reinforced by the use of tropes of the nation as body and the city as its nerve-centre.

From the start, this was a discourse that referenced itself all the time. Books quote freely from each other, creating and mutually reinforcing a growing sense of apocalyptic inevitability. In *The Citizen Faces War* (1936) the authors are so sure of their ground that they need only to recapitulate its key features in brief to call on a whole interrelated web of moral and political ideas. Despite the development of more realistic thinking, they are still thinking in terms of a 'knock-out blow'. And again the effects of bombing are presented through a trope of visualisation.

> That is the picture we have to face – the picture of such a packed, stampeding crowd of city-dwellers, flying without hope of getting clear, dying part of it in the shambles, part of it out at last, and presently struggling and fighting again to get food, as food grows ever scarcer; dying now of hunger and exposure and wounds and disease, and at the hands of desperate men. The breakdown of our civilisation – is that an idle phrase today?

Far from an idle phrase, it was on everyone's lips in the 1930s, and the subject of plenty of novels as well as non-fiction tracts. Whether it was to come about through war, or economic or political catastrophe, the future of civilisation was an almost universal concern. It seemed to many that capitalism was in the last stages of collapse, and would need to be replaced, peacefully or violently, by another system. Inseparable from this was a series of other important questions: what was civilisation? what did it consist of? how could it be measured, or assessed, or recorded? If it was widely agreed that the world was facing a crisis, was the present state of civilisation to blame? Or was it under threat from less civilised, or even totally uncivilised, forces? What did ordinary citizens in the USA or western Europe stand to lose, and from whom, and how?

Questions, answers and explanations proliferated. It was the age of global solutions like Communism and Fascism, as well as economic, social and political alternatives like the Social Credit movement, the Peace Pledge Union, sex reform,

Moral Rearmament, sunbathing, psychoanalysis and vege-
tarianism. It was a time of extreme intellectual ferment, with
greater quantities of argumentation in print than ever before.
There was a huge need for documentation – not merely the
kind of statistical information which had been so important
to reformers and rulers in the previous century, but also testimony, evidence, a sense of what the world meant to other
people. The rapid growth in documentary writing and, more
influentially, of newsreel and documentary film exposed
large numbers of people to the experience of other sorts of
people for the first time in their lives. The consequences of
civilisation were there for all to see, in the distressed areas
of South Wales, Tyneside or Lancashire, or in the menacing
behaviour of foreign political leaders, or in the faces of refugees. There seems to have been a degree of anxiety which
was capable of attaching itself to almost anything. For many,
the future must have felt close, unpredictable and threatening. In those circumstances, people's worries fed off visions
of disaster which in their turn drew sustenance and new
power from the anxieties they caused. Yet, as one reviewer of
Heinz Liepmann's 1937 novel *Death from the Skies* (published
in the USA as *Poison in the Air*) percipiently pointed out, 'The
anticipation of death and chaos through war is in a horrible
way exciting too.'

One element central to this idea of the breakdown of civilisation was the Frankensteinian paradox of science. Aviation,
as in the film *Things to Come*, might be the bringer of both
doom and salvation. The journalist Sisley Huddleston, in
War Unless ... (1933), succeeded in bringing most of the rel-
evant clichés together into one succinct formulation, when
he described aeroplanes as 'these wings over the world
[which] should bind land to land; but they may become

dark shadows over the earth'. The shorthand metonymy of wings recurs throughout the period, even lending occasional menace to political opinion, as in Wyndham Lewis's *Left Wings Over Europe* (1936). An intrinsic part of the glamour of the air was the fact that it had a darker side. Most objects of fascination are at least potentially dangerous, but the aeroplane was the apotheosis of both. From the earliest days of flight, it had been a symbol of the future, and those regimes which saw themselves embracing or conquering or reshaping the future made the aeroplane central to their self-image. 'Air-mindedness' captured the public imagination of Europe and America. Huge amounts of money were poured into the aircraft industry, and new models appeared in fierce competition and with great rapidity. The English Channel, then the Atlantic, was crossed by air. Non-stop flights became longer and longer. Air races, with large prizes, such as the Schneider Trophy, were endowed, by newspapers, monarchs, industrialists and duchesses. Distance, speed and endurance records were set and broken. Journeys became more adventurous. Airmen, and airwomen, flew to the Far East, to Australia, and round the globe, and became national heroes. And, as Azar Gat has pointed out, the long-distance flights of Italian aeronautical heroes like Italo Balbo had a dual purpose: both to 'foster Fascism's image as an advanced, dynamic, and virile movement' and also to test the feasibility of strategic bombing.

Air triumphs and catastrophes were a favourite subject of film and newsreel, and in Germany and Italy particularly advances in aviation were seen as central to the state's image. As Michael Paris explains, 'Cinematic demonstrations of aeronautical progress generally followed one of two basic forms. The state revealed itself as technically advanced, firstly through a focus on the heroic qualities of aviators, on epic or record-breaking flights or on the superiority of new machines, and secondly through imposing images of the nation's air power and preparations for defence against aerial bombardment.' (The latter became increasingly important towards the end of the 1930s.) 'The Nazis,' says Peter Fritzsche in his intriguing study of German aviation and the popular imagination, 'made the revival of German aviation an effective allegory for their own movement,' and made extensive use of planes and airships for propaganda purposes. He describes how first the building of the vast airship the *Hindenburg*, then its triumphal flight with the *Graf Zeppelin* over the German countryside in 1936, impressed its observers with a deep sense of the power and the all-seeing nature of the Nazi Party. The aestheticisation of air transport, and of the speed and power of aircraft, became an important element in the Nazi Party's appeal. The opening sequence of Leni Riefenstahl's film *Triumph of the Will* (1935) shows Hitler descending through the clouds in an aeroplane. After Hitler renounced the Treaty of Versailles in March 1935, and started openly to build up the Luftwaffe (previously disguised as the 'German League of Sportsflyers'), air shows and demonstrations of air power were frequent spectacles, as they were at the Berlin Olympics or at Nazi Party rallies, and they played an important part in persuading visitors and political commentators that the German air force was larger and stronger than it actually was. The rearmament programme was dramatised in Riefenstahl's film *Day of Freedom* (1935), which featured the popular air ace Ernst Udet dive-bombing a power station.

Along with mountaineers (another Riefenstahl image), aviators, pilots and their machines represented the triumph of man over nature, of machine over the natural barriers of sea, desert, jungle and mountain, and more than anything else put qualities of courage, determination, modernity and will at the centre of cultural attention. Lone figures conquered snowbound peaks, as if the world could be put right by relying on the same qualities. Unfortunately these qualities were also the contested ideals of Fascism and Communism. One of the most eloquent statements is Le Corbusier's excitable 1935 compilation of texts and photographs on the 'epic of the air', simply titled *Aircraft*. 'Today,' he says in the introduction, 'it is a question of the airplane eye, of the mind with which the Bird's Eye View has endowed us; of that eye which now looks with alarm at the places where we live ... The airplane eye reveals a spectacle of collapse.' Le Corbusier – architect and town planner – looks down on cities and wants to destroy them: 'Cities must be extricated from their misery, come what may. Whole quarters of them must be destroyed and new cities built.' He imagines a new consciousness, which in fact is very like the existing consciousness of totalitarianism. Metaphor and reality are alarmingly intertwined.

But this public, celebrity face of flying – the world of Lindbergh, Italo Balbo, Saint-Exupéry and Amy Johnson; of flying boats and high-speed racers – reflected, and masked, a complex mix of technology, design, manufacture, and commercial and state policy, with the same aircraft used for advertising, propaganda, travel, trade, menace, pride and war. Many historians have pointed out the binary consequence of flight: that speed and accessibility, with all their wonderful advantages in shrinking the globe and creating conditions for a world community, simultaneously created the threat of complete destruction for those below, and encouraged states to rearm, to terrorise and discipline their civilian populations, and to organise their defences. Similarly, the rapid development of air warfare was paralleled by an international movement for air disarmament, attempts to establish an international air police, and other pacifist or 'rational' schemes. Both attitudes – enthusiasm and fear – were shared, consciously or unconsciously, by almost everyone.

But, as David Edgerton has argued, there was no clear scientific reason for the English state to choose the aeroplane as its 'key strategic technology'. Colonial policing experience, he writes, had

> suggested that it was a cheap method of warfare. But just as important [I would argue more important] was a general overestimation of the power of the bomber to bring an industrial nation to its knees. Some of this was due to the propagandist enthusiasm of the air power advocates, but the effectiveness of their arguments was in part due to the way such feelings resonated with broader currents of popular opinion in the interwar years. Among these were fears for the stability of industrial societies and the desire to find new heroes for an unheroic age.

Perhaps because it lagged far behind Britain in the acquisition and development of technology, but far outstripped it in rhetorical extravagance, Italy seems to have been the most fruitful ground for the early development of these ideas. Filippo Marinetti's 1909 'Futurist Manifesto', adopting a tone of aristocratic scorn for conventional values, sang the praises of velocity, machinery, and war, 'war – the only hygiene of the world, militarism, patriotism ... and scorn for women'. England's own avant-garde artist Wyndham Lewis (who was never keen to be upstaged) countered this absurd macho rhetoric with a positive dislike of speed, and some patronising comments about Marinetti's infatuation with machines. 'You are always exploding about internal combustion. We've had machines here in England for donkey's years. They're no novelty to *us*.' They were, on the other hand, the stimulus to writers such as H. G. Wells, and Wells's vision of the future, like Jules Verne's, underlay Futurism, and the idea of a new political and technocratic élite derived from figures like Gabriele d'Annunzio.

Almost from the beginning, the idea of aerial bombardment was inextricable from fantasy and the literary imagination, but, of all the writers and artists associated with Italian Futurism, it was a military figure on the fringes of the movement who had the most profound influence in popularising the idea of air warfare as heroic, cataclysmic and decisive. Giulio Douhet (1869–1930), the most influential proponent of the idea of total warfare, was a career soldier, but also a novelist, a poet and rhetorician, a friend of Marinetti and d'Annunzio, and from its foundation in 1919 an enthusiastic supporter of Mussolini's Fascist movement. Outspoken and arrogant, he had broad interests that covered science and technology, with a particular focus on mechanisation and motor and air transport. But, whatever the subject occupying his mind, the thought that interested him above all was its application to the practice of warfare.

In 1921 he published his most influential book, *The Command of the Air*, an essay which incorporated and consolidated most previous thinking about air warfare, building on his own military experience for its confirmation. It rapidly achieved the status of a classic, despite not being translated into English until 1942. An unofficial English version was circulating in US air-training establishments as early as 1923: one of the leading, and most outspoken, US theorists of air warfare between the wars was Lieutenant-Colonel 'Billy' Mitchell, whose ideas were crucially shaped by both Trenchard and Douhet.

That Douhet's ideas so rapidly gained widespread adherence and were so influential on the policy of national air forces reflected the apocalyptic attitudes they expressed, and therefore the centrality they gave to national air forces. At the heart of his vision were three fundamental convictions: that war was inevitable, that attack was the only defence, and that any society would collapse completely if it was attacked from the air. This last belief was grounded on a minimum of scientific observation, extrapolated from the relatively small-scale raids of the First World War, but it seems to have articulated a very widely held fear, and to have done so with unusual persuasiveness, partly because Douhet was himself so fascinated with the artistic possibilities of his topic and so convinced of his own rightness.

An enthusiastic reader of H. G. Wells's visions of the future, which nourished his own activities as an amateur Futurist painter, writer, poet and playwright, Douhet was able to capture the imagination of his readers with a compelling series of deeply rhetorical arguments and apocalyptic accounts of destruction. Indeed, his last piece of writing, *The War of 19—*, commissioned by *Rivista aeronautica* and published in 1930, was a powerful fictional illustration of his theories in an account of war in the near future between defeated Germany and a Franco-Belgian alliance. The eighty-page novella was written, claimed Douhet, under a 'tight rein of logic and the straitjacket of reason', so it gave the impression of being a deeply considered vision of the future. But his approach had always been highly rhetorical. Azar Gat quotes from an extraordinary lecture that Douhet gave in Turin in 1913 – part poetry, part prose, glorifying the new age of air warfare. 'The bent wings / of men are passing … man and his / dreadful thunderbolt … The delicate machines were reset on the new homeland of Italy, leaving the light trail of their talons on the wet sand of our seas; like new human eagles they rose against the enemy …' In his subsequent writings through the 1920s, his rhetoric grew increasingly radical, as his vision of the future was incorporated more closely into the quasi-spiritual symbolisation of aeroplanes and flight in the Fascist political imaginary.

At the heart of *The Command of the Air* were two complementary arguments, both presented as fact. The first concerned the undeniable power of the aeroplane and the speed of its technological development. The second concerned civilian morale. Given the power of a pre-emptive bombing attack, nations and civilians were defenceless against it.

> No longer can a line of demarcation be drawn between belligerents and non-belligerents, because all citizens wherever they are can be victims of an enemy offensive … It seems paradoxical to some people that the final decision in future wars may be brought about by blows to the morale of the civilian population. But this is what the last war proved, and it will be verified in future wars with even more evidence. The outcome of the last war was only apparently brought about by military operations. In actual fact it was decided by the breakdown of morale among the defeated people – a moral collapse caused by the long attrition of the people involved in the struggle.

The spectre haunting his picture of destruction was not only the breakdown of civilian morale but also its consequences, the breakdown of the social order, the revolt of the people against their warmongering government in a general uprising to demand peace.

> By bombing the most vital civilian centres [an aggressor's airforce] could spread terror through the nation and quickly break down [its] material and moral resistance ... Within a few minutes some twenty tons of high-explosive, incendiary, and gas bombs would rain down ... As the hours passed and night advanced, the fires would spread while the poison gas paralysed all life ... A complete breakdown of the social structure cannot but take place in a country subjected to this merciless pounding from the air.

Although this vision of the collapsing moral fibre of a nation was, like most of his other beliefs, open to vigorous criticism, it was widely accepted in the interwar years. It was, as A. C. Grayling has pointed out, an attractive one to Arthur Harris, Hugh Trenchard and others in the RAF hierarchy. Their enthusiasm also had a strong racist component. The 'morally inferior' tribesmen of the Middle East, India and East Africa, as we have seen, responded to bombs with panic and disarray. The British, by contrast, were convinced that they were more likely even than other European peoples to stand firm in the face of bombs. (An equivalent conviction may have been shared by other nations too, of course.) Douhet's projected future had no real basis in technological fact, and would be largely disproved by the experience of the Second World War, for which it provided the blueprint. But its persistence points to something deeper than rational assessments and likely outcomes: it appealed to that profound fascination with the potential end of civilisation, even in some cases a desire for destruction, which fuelled such a wide range of imaginative productions throughout the modernist period, from 1910 to 1945. Actuality became less imperative in some quarters than notions of what could or might be.

In the mid-1930s, the worlds of fantasy, imperialism and military reality began to coincide. Mussolini's invasion of Abyssinia saw more aggressive and more experimental use of bombardment, with both gas and high explosive. The conflict had an additional attraction for newspapers and newsreels, as Mussolini's sons Vittorio and Bruno were both pilots in the 14th Bomber Squadron. Vittorio's comments on the joy of dropping bombs on horsemen and villages were immortalised in his memoir of the war, *Voli sulle ambe*, which was published in Florence in 1937 and in Munich in German translation almost immediately afterwards. Most famously he also, later, described the sight of bombed horsemen 'blooming like a rose when my fragmentation bombs fell in their midst. It was great fun.'

It was a brutal and one-sided conflict, and the incompetent haste with which Baldwin, Hoare and Eden rushed to appease the aggressor gave additional piquancy to the Italians' war crimes. The Italians systematically bombed Red Cross ambulances and hospitals, starting in December 1935. At the end of that month they killed twenty-seven patients and a Swedish volunteer medic at Dolo; three more camps were bombed and machine-gunned in January. Between 16 and 19 February, Italian planes, including Vittorio Mussolini's, dropped mustard gas on Ras Mulugeta's retreating Ethiopian troops and machine-gunned them as they tried to escape. Some fifteen thousand were killed or injured. Two weeks later a plane bombed a British Red Cross field unit in flat, open country near Quoram. For half an hour the plane flew back and forth, dropping incendiaries and high explosive on the clearly marked medical tents, including one bomb that hit the middle of the huge Red Cross flag spread out on the ground. Most of the unit was destroyed; five men were killed, and several more wounded. Vittorio Mussolini, the pilot, pretended in his memoir that he was shot at, and that the camp contained camouflaged gun emplacements. Marcel Junod, later president of the Red Cross, experienced a similar attack on 17 March, when his Red Cross plane, bringing supplies to the British camp, was bombed and set on fire. The whole area was bombed and gassed for some hours; the Italians had been dropping gas bombs and spraying gas every day for weeks. Junod describes seeing thousands of Ethiopians with 'horrible, suppurating burns'. The gas was yperite (mustard gas), a carcinogenic, clinging, oily liquid that attacked the eyeballs and lungs as well as blistering the skin.

All these attacks on humanitarian targets were deliberate policy, as G. L. Steer, reporting the war for *The Times*, saw all too clearly. 'The bombardment ... was cold-blooded and deliberate. It had the same object. It was intended to drive away the Red Crosses from the front while the Italians were employing illegal means of warfare. They now began to weave a web of gas all over Lake Ashangi and the plain of Korem.' The British government preferred to turn a blind eye, however, and even denied that there was any evidence of the Italian use of poison gas. When eventually it became impossible to ignore it any longer, it was too late. The only effect of Anthony Eden's address to the League of Nations in April 1936 was to raise fears at home even more. He pointed out that almost all countries had signed the 1925 Geneva Gas Protocol, and wondered, if nobody took any notice of it, how there could be any confidence that 'our own folk ... will not be burned, blinded and done to death in agony hereafter'. There could be none.

The fear of gas had been at the heart of the fear of bombardment since the war, and especially since the pronouncement in the House of Commons in 1927 that 'Our cities will not merely be decimated but rendered uninhabitable by chemical bombs ... We are faced with the wiping out of civilisation.' The most quoted comment was Lord Halsbury's in 1933: that a single gas bomb, 'if dropped on Piccadilly Circus, would kill everybody in an area from Regent's Park to the Thames', which amounted to about a million people. More rational counter-assessments failed to persuade a population eager for more meaty visions of catastrophe. In the 1920s, novels frequently included gas as an element in their doomsday scenario; but it was a pseudonymous 1931 novel, *The Gas War of 1940* by 'Miles' (reprinted under Stephen Southwold's more familiar pseudonym of Neil Bell), that really popularised the genre. The world has been effectively destroyed: 'The population of the world, which a week ago was roughly two thousand millions, is today little more than a quarter of that figure, and of these six hundred odd millions many are wounded, many sick, and many doomed, doomed as I am to die of their wounds, or from the pestilence that is raging with fury in every part of the world.' The novel concludes with the familiar argument that 'man has created a peril which he must now at all costs avoid. That peril is the perfection of instruments of destruction.' (There is an eloquent comment on altered anxiety priorities in the 1940 paperback reprint: exploiting the likely result of reading the book in bed, a full-page advertisement for the bedtime drink Bourn-vita is inserted into the Epilogue, facing the page I've just quoted from, with the heading 'Don't Let Worry Spoil Your Sleep ... Make Sound Sleep Your Daily Defence.')

CIVILIANS AND CIVILISATION

The definitive account of popular future-war fiction is the essay by Martin Ceadel in which he focuses his rich and sug-gestive analysis on some forty popular English novels pub-lished between the wars. He shows how the popularity of novels featuring airborne gas attacks increased in the early 1930s, at the same time as movements for peace and disarma-ment began to attract mass support, as fears grew of the pos-sibility of a 'knock-out blow' in a coming war. Disarmament, fear of rearmament, had been an important element in the Conservative defeat in the 1929 general election. That this immediately followed the high point of reminiscences and fiction about the First World War was not a coincidence.

Many people believed that an arms race and the entrenched positions that underlay it had been among the war's causes. This was especially the case after the announcement in 1931 that the World Disarmament Conference would finally convene the following year in Geneva. The recent upsurge of retrospective writing about the First World War, mainly in the form of memoirs and novels about infantry experience in the trenches, had raised the general consciousness of the horrors of war. After 1931 the present and the immediate future seemed more pressing concerns. The powerful descriptions of horrendous experiences published in the 1920s by Ford

Madox Ford (Hueffer), Richard Aldington, Robert Graves, Edmund Blunden, Siegfried Sassoon (all, incidentally, poets) and many others had created a new climate of awareness. As the international situation worsened, writers turned increasingly away from flimsy fantasies to pessimistic visions of the destructive potential of scientific invention, if it were not firmly controlled by responsible governments with enough political maturity to coexist peacefully with each other. In 1935, shortly before Italy invaded Abyssinia, the Peace Ballot, a poll of 11 million British people conducted by the League of Nations Union, voted overwhelmingly for international security through disarmament. Over 9 million voted in favour of the 'all-round abolition of national military and naval aircraft by international agreement'. In the *Left Review* of August 1935, the lead feature was a selection of war poems by Sassoon and Wilfred Owen as inspiration to writers in the current political situation. 'All the poet can do to-day,' as Owen said, 'is to warn.'

It is this cautionary note, especially about uncontrolled technology, which particularly marks the writing of this period. As Jonathan Griffin wrote in *Britain's Air Policy* in 1935, 'the new incendiary bomb has already made every private aeroplane a destructive and elusive weapon'. People were only too aware that new radio guidance techniques allowed pilots to bomb cities they couldn't even see. These almost metaphysical powers invited millennial fears. The threat of a sudden, silent and vast invasion of domestic airspace, and the destruction of London or some other major city, however practically improbable, was the most widespread and popular form these fears took. It should not be thought that all novels envisaged catastrophe, however. The *Decameron* format of *Zeppelin Nights* was used again in

1936, in an entertaining and intelligent novel of ideas called *Retreat from Armageddon* by Muriel Jaeger, in which a group of articulate professional people is invited to a house party at a Welsh farmhouse to escape the panic and destruction of long-expected air raids, and to await their fate. In the evenings they discuss things like the nature of civilisation and how to respond to the catastrophe. In the event the attack turns out not to have been catastrophic at all, its only ill effects being panic and demoralisation. Peace conferences are convened, and life continues as usual.

Following on from Lord Halsbury's *1944* (1926), the most influential novels that did dramatise the fear of extinction were Bernard Newman's *Armoured Doves* (1931), Ladbroke Black's *The Poison War* (1933), McIlraith and Connolly's *Invasion from the Air* (1934), *Air-Gods' Parade* (1935) by 'Simpson Stokes' (a pen name of the amazingly prolific Frank Fawcett), Leslie Pollard's *Menace* (also 1935), Joseph O'Neill's *Day of Wrath* (1936) (which imagines most of the world's cities destroyed with bombs containing poison gas, followed by thermite bombs which create firestorms), and L. E. O. Charlton's *War Over England* (1936). *Exodus A.D.* (1934), by Princess Paul Troubetzkoy and the painter C. R. W. Nevinson, subtitled 'A warning to civilians', carried Nevinson's horrific painting *Homo Sapiens* on the dust jacket, with a blurb advertising 'one of the most sensational novels of our time ... the collapse of civilisation and the terrifying, insane panic which follows the destruction of London from air attack'.

A range of earlier novels, including Oliver Baldwin's *Konyetz* (1924) and Shaw Desmond's *Ragnarok: A Novel of the Future* (1926), had dramatically portrayed the corruption of a bankrupt civilisation by Bolshevism, Jews or machines, and

14. *The searchlight image so widespread in First World War iconography and poetry is used again here on the dust jacket of Mass Observation's* War Begins at Home *in a stylised but immediately recognisable way at the start of the Second.*

its collapse into war, with bombs, poison gas, earthquakes and catastrophic destruction, but they reflected the bleak aftermath of the First World War and fear of social revolution or social upheaval, rather than any measured appraisal of a technological future. Their successor novels of the 1930s draw extensively on the arguments and projections of the 1920s within a much more acute consciousness of crisis, and a concomitant sense of the reality of a future war. *Menace* is typical in having a foreword by an air-vice marshal, who opportunistically stresses the need for a 'powerful air force' and writes that 'it would be a bold person indeed who would say that the main outline of the story is at all fantastic'. Its dust-jacket design also draws on familiar ideas, depicting a dark, prominently clawed eagle stooping through the clouds on its invisible prey. (The jacket also appeals to the documentary interests of its readers, promising a glimpse of 'all the interesting minutiae of an air pilot's life'.)

The most seriously intended of all the novels of future war was H. G. Wells's *The Shape of Things to Come* (1933); part fiction, part social analysis, this starts from the premise that a combination of the arms industry, the Versailles Treaty, the failure of the League of Nations and the breakdown of 'finance' result in a protracted war, with air bombardment, gas attacks, and finally germ warfare, and the complete collapse of civilisation. The book was followed by a film, *Things to Come* (1936), produced by Alexander Korda. It omitted, as it had to, all the book's speculative social theory, and dramatised the main narrative, with vivid scenes of gas panic and high-explosive bombing. It was this, rather than the redemptive conclusion in which the technocratic saviour descends from an aeroplane – no longer a symbol of destruction – which stayed in people's minds when they left the cinema.

By 1937 there was the additional evidence of Guernica. In *The Menace of the Clouds*, another warning by L. E. O. Charlton, published that year, the author seized on it to support his case, 'London will be at once attacked,' he wrote. 'To argue otherwise is lunacy; and, after the Guernica atrocity ... to assert that the law of humanity will prevail is to flout precedent in a proceeding that knows no law.' More and more books and pamphlets, some drawing on the Spanish experience, appeared demanding a more rapid, larger-scale and more realistic approach to air raid precautions (ARP). With extensive evidence from Spain of the nature and effect of

15. In this poster, pressurised water jets from the hosepipes of auxiliary firemen, rather than searchlight beams, provide the dramatic diagonals.

area bombing, the alarmist visions of gas warfare and total moral collapse could be tempered by practical arguments for better civilian defence against high explosive and incendiaries. In 1936 (incidentally, also the year of the first surrealist exhibition) the government announced that it was manufacturing 30 million respirators for free distribution. A group of Cambridge scientists published two reports into the inadequacy of the ARP measures proposed by the government; they also mounted public demonstrations (in King's Parade) of the effects of bombing, with actual models of buildings and blast damage. J. B. S. Haldane's *A.R.P.* (1938), in which the author pointed out the inefficiency of gas, explained that it hadn't been used in Spain because bombs were more effective, and argued for fewer anti-gas precautions and better defence against high explosives. The government, Haldane argued, had refused 'to face the facts of the Spanish war', and should now do so, before it was too late.

The rational case was hard to argue, however. The catastrophe predictions suited the arguments of the RAF because they strengthened its case for more money, men and machines. They suited the pacifists because the worse the threat, the more powerful their case for strategies of disarmament. And they suited the novelists because people really wanted to read about the apocalyptic collapse of civilisation. As Christopher Joel Simer has pointed out, 'scaremongering' was the preferred method of persuasion. But popular fiction, as we have seen, only recycled and reinforced the existing discourses of war. Martin Ceadel and Simer are both right in their accounts of the popular novel, but more serious literature fell explicitly outside the scope of their investigations. In the last part of this chapter I want to suggest some ways in which the same influences can be seen at work in poetry.

RAIDS ON THE INARTICULATE

A marked feature of poetry in the 1930s was an allegorical focus on Time as agency. History, crisis, revolution, the end of things as they were – all could be figured either as Time or more domestically as 'today' and 'tomorrow'. In some cases Time might be redemptive, as in Stephen Spender's poem 'From All These Events', where 'Time solitary will emerge / Like a rocket' and leave us 'untangled' from all the events and entanglements of life. This is very different from the Victorian novelists' idea of time as revealer and resolver:

this is a sudden transformational power, pointing optimistically towards revolution. In Charles Madge's 'Loss' we find a more conscious, even pensive, presentation of time:

> As in Vienna now, the wounded walls
> Silently speak, as deep in Austria
> The battered shape of man is without shade
>
> So, time in metaphor, tomorrow falls
> On Europe, Asia, and America,
> And houses vanish, even as they were made …

The sense that tomorrow, like a bomb, 'falls', rather than dawns, breaks or simply comes, permeates the writing of the mid-1930s. The confected optimism of the late 1920s and early 1930s, inspired by the idea of Communism and the largely imagined achievements of the Soviet Union, had succeeded in coexisting with the discourse of Armageddon. Where necessary, it had figured the final battle as one between progress and reaction, reversing the much more widespread vision of Communism, or the Jewish–Bolshevist conspiracy, as the greatest threat to civilisation. But, from 1933 onwards, Hitler's rise to power, the failed workers' uprising in Vienna, Mussolini's invasion of Abyssinia, Franco's revolt in Spain and Japan's aggression in China created a climate of crisis in which melodrama replaced the *Bildungsroman* as cultural paradigm. Strikingly, Rex Warner concluded a 1934 sonnet with an ultimatum which reassessed the natural progressions exemplified by seasonal change, and posed a starker choice – one which foreshadowed the later call to 'take sides':

> fearing for my fellows, for the murder of man.

How should I live then but as a kind of fungus,
or else as one in strict training for desperate war?

The year after that was written, the novelist Storm
Jameson argued that 'there are epochs when the artist has
enough to do copying out the actual forms of his world.
The sharpened senses of the artist of 1935 seem to feel
the pressure of forces which are still below the surface of
our world, working in it to change, perhaps to destroy it.
The note of warning, of uneasy fear, is persistent in all the
older serious writers.' This was characteristically percep-
tive. But it raises the question of how far that sense of
fear or unease can be attributed specifically to bombing,
or whether it would be more helpful to put the question
differently and to consider how far this fear of bombing
was created or intensified by other fears that are perhaps
present in everybody but that were given a specific inflec-
tion or form by the particular historical events of the 1930s,
especially the bombing of civilians. If, as psychoanalysis
suggests, our greatest fear is of ourselves, of something
terrifying inside us, does the emotional force of the fear of
death from the air derive from a projection of inner fears
on to the – already very threatening – outer world? Where
does the inside end and the outside begin? Where are our
borders, our frontiers?

It is a familiar observation that the concept or trope of the
frontier is an important motif in British writing of the 1930s,
and for good historical and geographical reasons, given the
changing maps of Europe and the Empire. As early as the
end of the First World War, Britain had ceased to be an island,
or at any rate people had stopped believing in the safety that
islandhood bestowed. Now that they could be bombed from

the air, islands were suddenly no less vulnerable than the mainland of Europe, the Middle East or Africa. The new permeability of what had been impassable frontiers, and the shift in the location of war from the 'front' to the 'area', paralleled the collapse of the distinction between combatant and civilian that aerial bombardment entailed. War as an affair of specialist armed forces gave way to total war. On 24 July 1924 Baldwin declared that 'the history of our insularity has ended, because with the advent of the aeroplane we are no longer an island' (a remark which Giulio Douhet soon quoted with glee).

But, beyond geography, the idea of the frontier was also used for articulating anxieties about definitions of class, race and gender, or about identity, separation, commitment and realignment. There was also a good deal of thinking about the borderline between inside and outside, from aesthetics (Adrian Stokes's *Colour and Form*) to fiction (Edward Upward's *Journey to the Border*) to politics. Soviet ideologue Karl Radek hit out against European modernism (in this case, James Joyce) at the 1934 Congress of Soviet Writers, by insisting that 'we must turn the artist away from his inside, turn his eyes to these great facts of reality which threaten to crash down on our heads', implicitly reminding us again of the inseparability of the two. This reality about to crash down on our heads had hitherto been beyond the oldest frontier: the frontier between earth and sky, between gods and man, now suddenly conspicuous by its absence. The collapse of the symbolic frontier of the sky that accompanied the technology of aerial bombardment also collapsed the frontier between civilian and military, between battlefield and the security of the home. What did time mean in this context? Was there a future? A violence that can descend in no time, from nowhere, from the empty sky, bringing with it limitless destruction, might also be a way of expressing a person's own unconscious violence.

Poets struggled to bring this sort of thinking into their work. H. B. Mallalieu, trying to come to terms with the bombing of Guernica, was acutely aware that the frontier with the future was ominously close; in 'The Future is Near Us' he wrote that

> The grey bomber has set limits to the air.
> Distance is death now and the carrier seas
> Hurl on these cliffs the message of despair.
>
> Spain has changed the contours of the Earth,
> Imposed new frontiers ...

The compression of this poem may be as simple as a school-boy code, but the simultaneous presence of all these concepts – frontiers, bombing, altered geography, death – points to a larger and more complicated pattern of discourse underlying it. The greater abstraction of poetry, or the abstracted distance in the work of novelists like Edward Upward or Rex Warner, means that these issues are not confronted directly, but that the writing tries to find ways to come at them obliquely, to fathom their depths and implications, or examine their consequences.

When the actual world becomes a melodrama, however, it is hard for writing to avoid sentimentality. Indeed, the kind of simplification of complicated issues that this implies can often be found in the intellectually dominant poetry of the 1930s, the Audenesque, despite the cloaks of irony that attempt to disguise it. The desire to speak out in poetry, to assert a political belief, or simply to voice an opinion as a citizen, could be urgent. Inner fear and aggression and an anxiety about the self can foreclose engagement with the nature and implications of the threatened violence, and import the violence into the verse, even in the form of a violent simplicity. The melodrama of the crisis of civilisation sidelined the problematic interplay of poetic language and social discourse which modernist writing had been exploring, in favour of a more knowing participatory or observational tone, but this also sometimes obscured the complex reasons underlying the melodramatic situation itself. The whole political culture of the interwar years operated within a melodramatic framework, with a polarisation between good and evil, civilisation and barbarism, Left and Right, and an overwhelming sense of imminent and mortal crisis. When people chose to 'take sides' in this struggle, they were opting to be agents of larger, invisible forces, and were committing themselves to the hands of History. The process of responding publicly and politically to the threat of annihilation by gas or bombs from the air paradoxically also made people powerless. And that tended to intensify the millenarian rhetoric, and increasingly the sense of the inevitability of war.

I. F. Clarke, who published a definitive account of future-war literature in 1966, argued that 'the entire literature of imaginary warfare is in the last analysis a myth-world created out of animosities and anxieties, and the whole projected into a fantasy of the future where only the worst or the best can come to pass'. If this is true, as I think it is, it raises a simple and basic question: why do people enjoy imagining the worst? Perhaps we can approach an answer to this via one of the earliest publications of the 1930s, Freud's essay *Das Unbehagen in der Kultur*, literally meaning 'unease in civilisation' but translated into English as *Civilisation and its Discontents*. (I want to retain the sense of unease here, remembering that 'uneasy' was the word used by Storm Jameson.) One of the recurrent themes in writing about bomb attacks, whether as a technical proponent or as an imagined victim, was, as we have seen, the certainty of social breakdown. Hit by bombs or gas, people, especially the lower classes, would 'maraud', 'riot', 'run amok' – in other terms, they would escape the repression that keeps their aggression or their libidinal energy within acceptable bounds. Freud's analysis of what civilisation means and what sustains it is, in Leo Bersani's words, a 'real and profound' reflection on aggression. Civilisation is necessarily built on the repression of our drives, but we are unhappy or uneasy because we have to restrain 'the extraordinarily high degree of narcissistic enjoyment' that satisfied aggression brings with it. Love and destructiveness are interlinked. Freud's account of the civilising process contains a basic contradiction.

In Bersani's brilliant reformulation, civilisation 'is merely a cultural metaphor for the psychic fulfilment in each of us of a narcissistically thrilling wish to destroy the world, a wish "fulfilled" in a monstrously ingenious phantasmatic scenario of self-destruction'. Civilisation and aggression are symbiotic. The melodramatic bombing scenarios so frequently repeated had a libidinal charge, as some writers were well aware. The thrills promised by popular novels stemmed from the simultaneous fear of and wish for the chaos unleashed by bombing. The contradictions may be less immediately apparent in more serious writing, but they are equally present – as they are for example in Auden's apparently stoical wish (in 'A Summer Night', 1933) for his culture to be swallowed up in the 'crumpling flood' of a new Communist society, an outcome which at the same time of course he is unable to envisage, let alone desire, at all. Or in Marion Milner's introspective essay *A Life of One's Own* (published under the pseudonym of 'Joanna Field' in 1934), in which she identifies her fear of death as a 'fear that my identity would be swallowed up'.

This was, to say the least, a complex situation, and it is not surprising that it precipitated so much projection. In the presence of all this violence and counter-violence, the question of death and people's relation to it became crucial. But of course, as Freud pointed out, our own death is not representable. By representing it, we transform it into spectacle and ourselves into spectators and therefore survivors. It is unspeakable, unimaginable – like the destruction of the world, or the void, the absolute chaos that follows. But, just as torture victims tell their torturers what they want to hear, fiction and non-fiction writers of the 1930s created a proliferation of versions of the same horrors, often almost in the same words, regardless of their ostensible purpose. There was no escaping them, even in dreams. Only when war was actually declared in 1939, according to Mass-Observers, did people's nightmares about a future cataclysmic conflict vanish.

3

WAR BEGINS AT HOME

'SUSPENSE WITHIN SUSPENSE'

Fantasies of future war, especially the earlier ones, rechan-
nelled existing fears and gave them a new and thrilling rationale. Fear of Jews, especially in the wake of
late-nineteenth- and early-twentieth-century immigration,
and fear of the working class, especially after the Russian
Revolution of 1917, both intensified the fear of invasion
which had been around since the 1870s. All these fears drew
on what are now well-documented new psychologies of the
city and the urban crowd. London was the largest great city
in the world, with a population in the late 1930s of 8 million,
and its inhabitants felt more than usually vulnerable to all
sorts of invasion, whether from disorderly crowds, stran-
gers, fire, bombs, gas or disease.

Much of the writing examined in the previous chapter
raised expectations of disaster by insisting that the world
was in a completely new situation, that apocalypse was a
real possibility, and that what people knew as civilisation
(however they thought of it) was only a thin veneer of
order restraining fathomless depths of chaos and hostility.
Psychologists told them that individuals were no different.
By the later 1930s people were just waiting for the frontiers
to be overrun. The way that Auden's trope of the 'crumpling

flood' was developed by C. Day Lewis in his verse play *Noah and the Waters* (1936), which dramatises the choice Noah has to make 'between clinging to his old life and trusting himself to the Flood', was symptomatic of the difficulty people had, even before Guernica, in thinking optimistically about future change. Now that the Condor Legion's attack on Guernica had demonstrated that an undefended town that constituted no military target could indeed be completely destroyed, and the action shrugged off or denied, the fear was shown to be completely grounded. As such, the conduct it represented raised, even more acutely than before, questions about the ethical and moral issues involved in modern warfare, the kinds of power it represented, and the kinds of social and political attitudes associated with it.

This can be seen, for example, in the complex treatment of these problematic issues in Rex Warner's novel, *The Aerodrome*, published in 1941 but largely written before the war started. The novel has allegorical elements, but is much more flexible in its psychology and its concepts than the term 'allegory' implies, and the juxtaposition of the two worlds of the Village and the Aerodrome – both, as Warner puts it in an author's note, 'somewhat repulsive' – provides scope for exploring issues such as the impact of air power and its associated politics on traditional cultural values. In the figure of the Air Vice-Marshal, and his insistence on the airman's abandonment of home, parents, locality and fatherhood, Warner is also able to give shape to a fascist outlook both alarming and believable. It is one of the few novels to tackle the real difficulty of engaging with the new outlooks and technologies of air-mindedness without resort to melodrama, hectoring or self-indulgence, but without dismissing their attractions either.

A new note of realism descended on the debate as the 1930s drew to a close, and the Munich crisis made war seem urgent and inevitable. The practical preparations for war and the visible signs of air-raid precautions like gas masks and sandbags brought an element of resignation and matter-of-factness to the idea of bombing. George Bowling, in Orwell's *Coming Up for Air* (1939), illustrates this well. Bowling's attempt to rediscover the way of life he knew as a child has failed. 'The old life's finished, and to go back looking for it is just a waste of time.' He recognises, in his way, that some basic change has occurred in the nature of civilisation, but doesn't react against that recognition. It is a bomb, accidentally dropped from an RAF plane on to a greengrocer's shop, that settles things for him.

> War is coming ... It's all going to happen. All the things you've got at the back of your mind, the things you're terrified of, the things that you tell yourself are just a nightmare or only happen in foreign countries. The bombs, the food-queues, the rubber truncheons, the barbed wire, the coloured shirts, the slogans, the enormous faces, the machine-guns squirting out of bedroom windows. It's all going to happen ... There's no escape.

When war was declared, the expected knock-out blow did not come. J. F. C. Fuller's prediction that London would turn into a 'vast raving Bedlam' in which people stormed the hospitals, the homeless shrieked for help, and all was 'pandemonium' remained dramatically unfulfilled. His was not a lone voice: the government had been expecting a quarter of a million dead in the first three weeks of war as a result of bombing, with up to half of London's remaining population pouring from the destroyed city into the countryside, homeless refugees. The psychiatric toll was expected to be enormous, with perhaps 3 million people driven out of their minds with terror. It was the existence of worst-case scenarios like these, coupled with the constellation of unsupported ideas about aerial attack we saw in the last chapter, that persuaded Chamberlain to reach an agreement with Hitler at Munich. He was, as Wesley Wark has put it, 'outdeterred'. Government departments, however, tried not to publicise these figures, in case the panic happened too early. Instead, they issued a steady stream of orders, relocated departments and offices, issued ARP leaflets, and provided local authorities with a million extra death-certificate forms.

So many of the fears associated with bombing seemed to have been absorbed into a growing bureaucracy, as belated efforts were made to prepare the country, especially London, for the onslaught. A better analogy for the situation than Fuller's might be Henry Green's group of young people in *Party Going* (1939); immobilised at Victoria station by thick fog, they look down from the windows of the railway hotel at the crowds 'underneath', sensing the injustice and precariousness of their social elevation. Jammed together like tailors' dummies, the people in the crowd are resigned but anxious. 'What targets for a bomb,' one of them remarks.

To avoid turning people into targets, zigzag trenches were dug in the London parks, and even across the sacred lawns of Oxford and Cambridge colleges. Free Anderson shelters were put in place in thousands of back gardens. The basement corridors of Buckingham Palace were strengthened and converted to shelters. Air-raid wardens were recruited. Just before the declaration of war, 1.5 million children were evacuated to the country, mostly from London. But the expected strike failed to materialise. Nothing happened. Instead of chaos and calamity there was bureaucracy and blackout. It was an entirely different sort of annihilation that Malcolm Muggeridge described at the end of his book *The Thirties*. 'Buildings sprouted sand-bags ... children were evacuated, cinemas closed, lights put out, London left dark, childless, cinemaless, at night scarcely existing at all, obliterated.' In this phoney-war emptiness, preparations were being made for war in the air. And as the Allies did not yet have the capability to attack Germany from the air successfully, they had to prepare to defend British cities against German bombers. One popular novel stands out at this point as countering the more extreme visions of what might happen. A more than usually informed, realistic and persuasive account of what was likely to happen in the event of a bomb attack, Nevil Shute's novel *What Happened to the Corbetts* was issued by the publisher in a special edition of a thousand copies for ARP personnel. In it Shute, who had worked in the aircraft industry all through the 1930s and had a well-informed idea of how air warfare was likely to develop, showed the probable consequences of high explosive and incendiary bombs on a provincial city. It may have had some success in ARP circles in helping to reduce the expectation of gas.

On 1 September 1939 – the same day that Auden was castigating the 'low dishonest decade', thinking about how 'Waves of anger and fear / Circulate over the bright / And darkened lands of the earth, / Obsessing our private lives' – President Roosevelt went on the radio with a speech in which he exhorted the European powers to refrain from bombing 'civilian populations or unfortified cities'. He called for an immediate response. Chamberlain responded positively, as did the French. Hitler replied that the idea 'corresponds completely with my own point of view', and set about bombing Warsaw. In the House of Commons on 14 September, Chamberlain reiterated his standpoint. The government would never, he declared, 'resort to the deliberate attack on women and children and other civilians for the purpose of mere terrorism'. Weasel words, in a way. The excuse given by the Japanese in China and by Franco's spokesmen in Spain was that no raids were ever carried out for 'mere terrorism', because there was always a military target. Even Guernica was sometimes claimed to have been a military target. It is not hard for governments or military authorities to provide meretricious justification for their acts of terror, if they think the acts of terror will be effective.

When war was declared, everyone breathed a sigh of relief that the period of uncertainty and waiting was over. Many expected that they would shortly be dead, and were puzzled that the anticipated apocalypse didn't come. An air of unreality was reported by many Mass-Observers. 'Everything seemed even more unreal; the wireless giving special announcements about air raids and the closing of cinemas, but the sun was still shining ... I felt as though there should be *something obviously different* – bad storms or something like that.' People guiltily hoped for something sensational. That some at least of the same emotions were still present even when British forces were getting ready to evacuate northern France in May 1940 is evident from the headlines that greeted the Luftwaffe's bombing of Rotterdam on the night of 14 May. Richthofen's bombers – fifty-seven Heinkel He-111s of the sort that had bombed Guernica – reduced the centre of the old city to ruins and killed nine hundred civilians, prompting the city's surrender. Newspapers everywhere next day condemned the attack as an act of barbarism, exaggerated headlines claiming as many as thirty thousand dead. Both terrifying and strangely welcome, it seemed at last to be a demonstration of what everybody knew was possible: unfettered, apocalyptic, air warfare.

The RAF's first bombing raids over Germany in September 1939 had been to drop propaganda leaflets, in the unlikely hope that the civilian population would see the error of their ways and call for peace. They didn't, nor did the presence of the British bombers have any noticeable effect on the life of the cities beneath. It was useful practice for the bomber crews, however. The other targets of the bombers in the first few months of the war were German warships, but the losses suffered when the daylight raids encountered German fighters caused a change of policy, and bombing raids thenceforth were nocturnal activities.

Meanwhile, nothing much was happening on the home front. The atmosphere of that first autumn of war is brilliantly caught in a poem David Gascoyne wrote in October 1939, 'An Autumn Park':

Dark suffocates the world; but such
Ubiquity of shadow is unequal. Here
At the spiked gates which crown the hill begins
A reign as of suspense within suspense:
Outside our area of sandbagged mansions and of tense
But inarticulate expectancy of roars,
The unhistoric park
Extends indifference through all its air.

Charles Madge and Tom Harrisson, in Mass-Observation's *War Begins at Home*, scathingly cite a newspaper account of a letter sent by Chamberlain to be read out at 'a luncheon' at the Dorchester. 'People are apt to get a little restive when, as they put it, nothing happens. So I welcome these luncheons … They will, I am sure, have a steadying effect on morale on the home front.' The 'bewildered' Chamberlain may have thought that a few words to the section of the civilian population that lunched at the Dorchester were enough to keep everyone's spirits up, but the two authors are far from convinced. They set out very powerfully the need to gather enough documentary information to be able to discover and analyse the 'complex pattern' of conflicting and contradictory attitudes and emotions which underlie the general civilian state of mind. This is the first war without frontiers, involving all the people at home as well as in the armed forces. 'In no war have the people been so materially concerned on such a massive scale. Progress and science have brought the shadow of the bomb over every family.'

The emphasis on progress and science was not ironic, even if the situation itself was. It was soon clear that the most important work of the home front would be the manufacture of aeroplanes – a process which later in the war provided an opportunity for some wonderful works of fiction or imaginative reportage, like Inez Holden's *Night Shift* (1941), Mark Benney's *Over to Bombers* (1943) and Diana Murray Hill's *Ladies May Now Leave Their Machines* (1944). The pause before bombing raids were launched by either side provided some time for work on aircraft design and for the production of new models to move forward. One of the first things Churchill did when he became prime minister in May 1940 was to set up a Ministry of Aircraft Production under Lord Beaverbrook. Earlier in the new year, on 27 January, he had made a rather disingenuous speech in Manchester.

I have no doubt that from time to time you ask yourselves the question, 'why is it that we have not yet been
attacked from the air?' Why is it that those severe ordeals
for which we had braced ourselves on the outbreak of war
have not been imposed on us during these five months?
… Is it that they are saving up for some orgy of frightfulness which will soon come upon us, or is it because so far
they have not dared? Is it because they dread the superior quality of our fighting aircraft? Is it because they
have feared the massive counterstroke which they would
immediately receive from our powerful bombing force?
No one can say for certain. But one thing is sure. It is not
from any sense of delicacy that they have refrained from
subjecting us to this new and odious form of attack.

This may usefully have talked up the state of Britain's air
force, but its chivalric tone was less than justified. It soon
transpired that Britain did not have a sense of delicacy
either. David Edgerton has shown how central the idea of
bombardment was to the British military and the British
government, and how crucially it was driven by a faith in
technology, while 'the public were deliberately misled as to
the aims of wartime bombing'. The fighter planes may have
held the headlines, but Churchill, as we have seen, had been
an advocate of strategic bombing for nearly thirty years, and
was not about to change his mind about its efficacy.

The early bombing campaign against Germany was not
a success, despite its intensity. Britain began bombing the
Ruhr in May 1940, after the German bombing of Rotterdam,
and between August that year and the following May it
dropped twenty thousand tonnes of bombs on Germany.
Germany dropped fifty thousand tonnes on England. But,

while the German bombing led to forty thousand casualties, the British only inflicted three thousand casualties on the Germans. Nevertheless, the commitment to strategic bombing grew stronger.

THE BLITZ

It is difficult to avoid using clichés to describe the experience of being bombed. Many of the contemporary accounts of the Blitz almost seem to make a virtue out it, welcoming the sense of dull repetition that the clichés bring with them. Many of the best, most imaginatively convincing, accounts are either about work – by firemen like Henry Green or William Sansom, or by air-raid wardens like John Strachey – or else describe situations where the bombing is in some sense oblique. As G. W. Stonier put it (in *Shaving Through the Blitz*, 1943), 'London has been given over to a monstrous drama, an act of darkness from which ordinary people, you and I as individuals, shut ourselves away.' There's a very good piece called 'Delayed Action' by Robert Herring in the November 1940 issue of the magazine he edited, *Life and Letters Today*, in which, in addition to a vivid description of daily life during the Blitz, and thoughts about the words he can use to describe it, he also writes about the effect on the self – the 'raid-like gaps' in his mind, the way that 'skulking in shelters, one is not one's self ... Working, one is. It is not being one's self that frightens.' This is something explored in the best Blitz novel, James Hanley's *No Directions* (1942), which culminates in an extraordinary attempt to create a sufficiently intense reaction to the sublime of bombardment.

The German attack on London started on 7 September 1940, and continued every night and often in daylight too for the next fifty-seven days. Most nights, between 200 and 350 tonnes of explosive were dropped on the city (up to ten times the weight of bombs dropped over Guernica). After that, although not quite daily, the bombing continued for another six months, until the final raid on 11 May 1941. Just over twenty thousand civilians died in London, and twenty-three thousand more across the UK. The popular 'myth of the Blitz' in which people cheerily announced that 'they could take it' was not entirely untrue, but certain other responses also need to be noted. Some 2 million members of the middle classes – those who were able to afford to – had moved out of London before the bombing began. Thousands of people in the East End forcibly occupied factory and ware-house basements and similar makeshift shelters, as well as Underground stations, in protest against the inadequate offi-cial provision. (You couldn't put up an Anderson shelter in a block of flats.) All it took to defy the government's policy on keeping the Underground stations clear was a penny-half-penny ticket – the police were not going to drive people back out into the middle of a raid. By the end of September, when the Tube night-time population hit its peak, there were esti-mated to be 177,000 shelterers.

The nightly life in one of the other occupied shelters, christened 'Underground City', and sounding very like the shelter off the Commercial Road in Stepney, in the winter of 1940, was vividly described by Jack Conrad in an issue of *Our Time*. A whole community is camped out there night after night for months. There is a powerful sense of working-class solidarity, and a general cheeriness, until one night there is a hit on the building above. People are thrown out of their bunks, the lights go out; everywhere is full of plaster and dust. 'Women become hysterical, children shriek in terror …

There is panic, panic in its most dangerous form.' Despite the clichéd prose, we are powerfully reminded that fear, even if, conventionally, mastered more quickly by men than by women, is present all the time, easily turning to panic and chaos. Vera Brittain describes an old man dropping dead of a heart attack at the sound of the sirens; Randall Swingler writes about a man going mad in the street after bombs had fallen nearby. 'People silent, alert in basements and shelters, heard him rave and scream about the square cursing Churchill, cursing the Government with every kind of obscenity, in a voice that echoed and carried for yards around. It was as if madness had stricken him with an overwhelming clarity of political vision. Unearthing perhaps a knowledge which sanity would never dare recognise.' Madness is sometimes necessary to turn things inside out so that they can be seen properly.

Stories proliferated – of narrow escapes, bizarre incidents, tragedies, comic incidents, and a general surreal twist on everyday reality. In her memoir of the early war years, *It Was Different at the Time* (1943), Inez Holden remembered how

one morning I walked back through the park, and saw the highest branches of a tree draped with bits of marabout, with some sort of silk, with two or three odd stockings and, wrapped round the top of the tree, like a cloak quick-thrown over the shoulder of some high-born hidaldo, some purple damask. Below it, balanced on a twig as if twirled round a finger, was a brand new bowler hat. They had all been blown across the road from the bombed hotel opposite. A surrealist painter whom I knew slightly was staring at this, too. He said: 'Of course we were painting this sort of thing years ago, but it has taken some time to get here.'

There is a brittleness to the blasé response that recognises and obliquely reveals the impulse to cover fear with whimsy or humour. Another typical story does something similar. Although large numbers of people did find shelter in public shelters and in the Tube, most preferred to stay at home, and William Sansom recounted an episode that was simultaneously terrifying and grotesquely comic. A delayed-action bomb fell on Sussex Street, in Westminster, and the inhabitants were all evacuated. At six in the morning the empty houses were blown into the sky. Or almost all of them. 'One man, a late night arrival, had climbed up unseen to his room and had gone to bed in sweet ignorance. He was lucky enough to have only half of his particular house blown away, and luckier still to have chosen to sleep in the half that remained.' He had to be rescued and brought down by ladder.

Audiences stuck in theatres or concert halls might enjoy (or endure) impromptu performances for two or three hours until the 'all clear' sounded. Rail and bus travellers got used to interruptions and slow journeys. And there were embarrassing episodes, as when a young woman in Poplar was having a bath when the house was hit by a bomb, and she was tipped upside down with the bath on top of her – much to the surprise of the rescuers, who when they lifted it up found an unharmed naked woman in the rubble. Vera Brittain said she never quite dared to take a bath during a raid. In her 1941 memoir of London in the summer and early autumn of 1940, *England's Hour*, she struggles to reconcile the heroism of ordinary people with her pacifist instincts which tell her how much more productively those energies might have been used in peacetime. She makes some important points. Recognising that 'death may descend upon any of us' at any time, she explores the nature of the fear this creates.

Coupled with the astonishing courage which surrounds us, the emotion that Amelia Earhart called 'the livid loneliness of fear' is now also [like heroism] a universal experience. How many men and women in this tiny country really listen with indifference to the hiccuping boom of the Nazi bomber as it passes overhead? The most conscientious of war propagandists need not despise this secret terror. Without it, 'civilian morale' would not be the outstanding achievement that it is.

But what, she is forced to ask, is it all for? What kind of civilisation is it that uses all this energy in the service of the state, to 'destroy another great nation'.

One of the most frequently repeated images of the Blitz – already almost a cliché when Orwell used it before the war in *Coming Up for Air* – was the two- or three-walled house, the building with its façade blown away revealing a domestic interior still intact, all of its private life exposed to the public gaze. As in the incident described by Inez Holden, what had been inside was revealed to the outside, almost as if the world was becoming an allegory of individual experience. Another frontier demolished. There's a wonderful photograph of such a ruin by Lee Miller. It provides an indication, should one still be needed, of how the locationless fear of bombing that characterised the 1930s, with its echo of the formless terrors within each person, was psychically reshaped by the shared experiences of the Blitz. As long as the bombing of cities was an impending threat, happening only somewhere else, to other people, in Spain or in China, it was capable of filling the imagination and creating almost limitless apprehension. When actual German planes started dropping high-explosive and incendiary bombs on London, the threat materialised, it became a reality shared with millions of other people. After a while it almost became dull. What had been exceptional became tolerable.

Eventually, later in the war, the whole idea of bombing began to merge with the 'aimlessness, sluggishness, voicelessness and moroseness' that Elizabeth Bowen remembered as an inescapable part of the post-Blitz years, when 'war moved from the horizon to the map'. But recollection, however apocryphal it seemed, still emphasised the communal aspect, which was such an unexpected feature of the Blitz (unexpected by politicians and government officials, at any rate). The intensity of emotions like fear was shared and externalised. Bowen makes two important points which help us understand how this happened. One is that the individual voice was externalised through the agency of the radio, of which she says that 'sound made for community of sensation'. The other is that she did not feel that she invented anything she wrote in her wartime stories. 'It seems to me,' she explained, 'that during the war the overcharged subconsciousnesses of everybody overflowed and merged,' so that her stories are 'saturated' with them, and possess 'an authority nothing to do with me'. This state of 'lucid abnormality' was not, for the most part, confronted with horrors sufficiently catastrophic to make it stop functioning, though Henry Green suggestively weaves traumatic forgetting into the texture of *Caught*, his 1943 novel about the Blitz.

Fire, rather than explosives, was what came to represent

the Blitz – in poems like Dylan Thomas's 'Ceremony After an Air Raid', Louis MacNeice's 'Brother Fire' and T. S. Eliot's 'Little Gidding'; in Humphrey Jennings's films and John Piper's and Leonard Rosoman's paintings; in countless photographs; in stories like Sansom's 'Fireman Flower'. Some poets, like C. Day Lewis in 'Word Over All' (1943), insisted that 'words there must be' to commemorate the devastation and heroism of those months, but were unable to find them. Day Lewis tries to take on the role of allegorist, but sinks beneath the weight of abstraction and gesture. The only section of the poem that works is in the third stanza:

> I watch when searchlights set the low cloud smoking
> Like acid on metal: I start
> At sirens, sweat to feel a whole town wince
> And thump, a terrified heart,
> Under the bomb-strokes ...

Other poets saw in the Blitz a culmination of science (a word that almost rhymes with 'sirens'), as in J. F. Hendry's 'Midnight Air-Raid', in which the 'white fire / From London's living furnace, flung up like a tilted cauldron, / Splits the atom of doom'. Yet, as Hubert Nicholson put it in 'Air Raid', when the fires are under control, and people resume their daily lives, 'they will smoke at the shattered window, saying "pro tem." / accepting the damaged world the dawn hands back to them'.

AREA BOMBING

Meanwhile, Bomber Command had been continuing to launch raids on German industrial cities, but with little to show for it. The raids were inaccurate, both in terms of navigation (the wrong location was often bombed) and accuracy (many bombs missed their targets). The disturbing discovery of an investigation in August 1941 was that, depending on visibility, only 7 to 40 per cent of bombs hit their targets. Regardless of visibility, only one-third of the planes to reach their designated targets managed to drop their bombs within five miles of it. But, reassured that new technologies being incorporated into the new bombers would improve both aspects, Churchill gave approval for Bomber Command to change its strategy. It was to move from its focus on naval and fuel targets to attacking and disrupting the transport network and 'destroying the morale of the civil population as a whole and of the industrial workers in particular'. Britain's policy now therefore embodied the approach that underlay the theories of Douhet and his followers. Destroying morale was inseparable from arousing fear and creating terror. Only euphemisms disguised the real purpose of the bombers. And under their new commander, Sir Arthur Harris, the campaign was purposeful.

In the summer of 1942, a leaflet was dropped over Germany, reminiscent of General Mola's threat to raze Vizcaya to the ground in 1937. It threatened the systematic and 'remorseless' bombing of all Germany's cities, and the people who lived and worked in them. Like the Luftwaffe in Spain, and in retaliation for the Blitz bombings of London and Coventry, Bomber Command was keen to experiment with fire. The bombers had already shown what they were capable of. Lübeck, their first target, in March 1942, was (like Guernica) full of old, half-timbered houses, and predictably went up in flames. Rostock followed over three nights in April. The Germans responded by bombing the 'Baedeker'

Heavy "Stirling" bombers raid the Nazi Baltic port of Lübeck and leave the docks ablaze

BACK THEM UP!

16. *This poster, depicting a successful air raid on Lübeck, also stresses the vulnerability of the bombers, which are seen from below, as a way of strengthening links between war work at home and the activities of Bomber Command.*

towns of Norwich, Bath, York and Exeter. On 30 May, nine hundred British bombers inflicted massive damage on Cologne, dropping over eight hundred tonnes of bombs and nearly a thousand incendiaries. The success of this raid gave Harris a basis to continue. Heavier bombers were entering production, and bombing, reconnaissance and navigation techniques were steadily improving, until by early 1944 there was an average of a thousand bombers a day available to Bomber Command. The other crucial element in this improved force was the arrival of large numbers of American bombers.

In his *Hitler and Spain*, Robert Whealey argued that 'Guernica served as a foretaste of the brutal inefficiency of so-called "strategic bombing", or rather the indiscriminate bombing of civilians, that marked World War II and the Korean and American–Indochina wars.' The term 'strategic bombing', as he implies, was no more than a propaganda tool. The wild inaccuracy of most bombing meant that most of the damage it caused could not be described as intentional. But the claim that it was strategic seemed to make the bombing part of a plan, gave it a higher purpose, so that the civilian deaths it necessarily entailed were somehow also excused. Vera Brittain was already making a similar point in her powerful 1944 pamphlet *Seed of Chaos: What Mass Bombing Really Means*, noting that 'the use of soporific words to soothe or divert the natural human emotions of horror and pity is a characteristic and disturbing feature of this war'. She prefers the term 'obliteration bombing'. Orwell reviewed her rather scathingly in his *Tribune* column, accusing her of illogicality and, implicitly at least, of bad faith. 'No one in his senses regards bombing … with anything but disgust,' he says, but he goes on to wonder why it's 'worse to kill civilians than soldiers'. It's a somewhat impatient, somewhat mischievous article, but one that has the force of pragmatism, as well as his usual sensitivity to linguistic humbug. It sparked off a debate that reflected a growing uncertainty in Britain about the use of area bombing, and about the feelings of vengeance and guilt associated with it. The most terrible success of the area-bombing campaign at the height of the war – and one about which Vera Brittain probably knew rather more than Orwell did – was the bombing of Hamburg and the firestorm it created on the night of 27 July 1943. The fact that it was called Operation Gomorrah makes its purpose clear enough. Ten thousand tonnes of high-explosive and incendiary bombs were dropped on densely populated residential areas. Within twenty minutes an enormous area of fires merged to form one single, vast, sea of fire. Air was sucked in by the heat at hurricane speeds, howling like a mighty organ, creating temperatures of eight hundred degrees and more. The fire reached two thousand yards into the sky and, in W. G. Sebald's summary, 'burned like this for three hours. At its height the storm lifted gables and roofs from buildings, flung rafters and entire advertising hoardings through the air, tore trees from the ground and drove human beings before it like living torches ... The water in some of the canals was ablaze.' People suffocated to death as they sheltered in the cellars, or sank into the bubbles of boiling tarmac.

Sebald's essay on 'Air War and Literature', in *On the Natural History of Destruction*, is a prolonged meditation on the inadequacy of most ordinary human language to communicate the experience of bombardment of this sort. 'The need to know was at odds with a desire to close down the senses.' Any attempt to describe horrors of this sort, as I argued earlier in relation to Guernica, can only make use of existing language and existing literary or artistic forms. Ostensibly eyewitness reports rehearse the same tropes, the same images, and sometimes the same errors. It is notoriously hard to recall traumatic experiences, and the sort of things people saw during and after bombardments were horrendous enough to begin with – the dismembered bodies thrown up by the first bombs to fall on Guernica, for example, scarcely warrant a mention beside the appalling events of Hamburg or Dresden, Tokyo or Hiroshima. The success of Picasso's painting, for all its modernist form, lies in the catalogue of recognisable symbols that constitute its narrative. Sebald states his argument in these terms: 'I do not doubt that there were and are memories of these nights of destruction; I simply do not trust the form – including the literary form – in which they are expressed.' The most precise and objective records are the most, if not the only, legitimate accounts. 'The construction of aesthetic or pseudo-aesthetic effects from the ruins of an annihilated world is a process depriving literature of its right to exist.' This ethical problem is one Sebald circumvents by quoting at length from the testimony he discusses. But the problem remains, and constitutes the permanent challenge to art and writing, to find a form equal to the material or the occasion.

The returning bombers could see the blaze from as much as 120 miles away. The destruction they had caused was unprecedented. Half the city was in ruins, and at least forty-five thousand civilians had been killed – more even than had died in the German bombing of Stalingrad the year before. Further attacks by the British and the Americans followed on other German cities: Hanover, Stuttgart, Münster, Osnabrück, Munich, Berlin and Dresden. The American strategy, on the whole, was to bomb fuel bases, factories and supply lines, in a more or less accurately targeted fashion, while the British – sometimes with American support – carried out indiscriminate area bombardments of cities. The attack that destroyed the baroque city of Dresden killed an unknown number of people in the firestorm it created – estimates vary from twenty-five thousand to six times that figure. It was the last major terror raid on Germany, though raids on other historic towns continued for a few more weeks. A. C. Grayling points out that when an RAF officer 'told a press briefing that the Allied Air Chiefs were employing a strategy of "deliberate terror bombing of German population centres as a ruthless expedient of hastening Hitler's doom", the words reached the front pages in the United States, but were censored in England'. On 28 March 1945, Churchill wrote to the chiefs of staff to say the time had come to review 'the question of bombing German cities for the sake of increasing the terror, though under other pretexts'.

JAPAN

The shape of the war had changed in June 1941, when the Germans had turned their attention eastward and attacked the Soviet Union. It changed again, in two ways, in December that year, when Japanese bombers attacked the US naval base at Pearl Harbor in a surprise precision strike targeted on the American fleet. This happened, by some profound irony, the day after the United States had officially decided to support the work already under way to develop the atomic bomb.

It was only in the last nine months of the war that Japan itself was bombed, in preparation for an anticipated seaborne invasion. The first attempts were high-altitude daylight

17. The irony of this merciful gesture as it takes in the destroyed city of Dresden once again uses the device of juxtaposition to make its point.

precision-bombing raids aimed at destroying Japanese air-craft and engine factories, but unexpectedly strong winds and poor visibility meant that these were largely unsuccess-ful. Not only did the winds blow the bombs off course, but at times they were strong enough to blow the planes them-selves backwards. Orders were therefore given to change to area bombing, and raids were planned on Nagoya, Osaka, Kawasaki and Tokyo. An experimental night raid was carried out over Tokyo in late February 1945, dropping a high proportion of incendiaries, and, while not a spectacular success, this did enough damage for the policy to be continued. Although Lewis Mumford described the adoption of saturation bombing techniques as a 'general moral disintegration' which culminated in the use of atomic weapons, the abandonment of strategic bombing and of an official reluctance to kill large numbers of civilians was more apparent than real. In reality, even the superior quality of its bombsights and radar had never allowed for the kind of precision that the USAAF claimed to achieve: much of the bombing carried out in Germany and initially in Japan had been area bombing in all but name. Nevertheless, the Americans' explicit intention was now to burn large numbers of people to death. Thomas Searle quotes Lieutenant-General Ira Eaker as saying 'It made a lot of sense to kill skilled workers,' echoing Lieutenant-General James Edmundson, who said that he had 'no compunction about participating in the fire bombing raids', as 'a lot of lives were saved, Japanese lives as well as American lives'.

However true this may have been, it was also only the latest form taken by the original Wellsian idea, adopted by Douhet, of the moral desirability of shortening wars by means of a 'knock-out blow'. The highly inflammable structures of many Japanese buildings, and their proximity to each other, made them a tempting target, and one likely to result in a devastating degree of destruction. In 1932, Brigadier-General 'Billy' Mitchell, one of the most outspoken American advocates of air power between the wars, had pointed out that 'incendiary projectiles would burn the cities to the ground in short order'. American experience in China in the late 1930s when the Japanese ruthlessly used incendiaries in their bombing of Chinese cities like Shanghai and Chungking, was not likely to encourage restraint either. The American attacks may not have been overtly racist, but the attitude to the Japanese that the USA demonstrated after Pearl Harbor suggests that a sense of its enemy's essential inferiority or inhumanity was a factor (as it has been since, in Korea, Vietnam, Afghanistan and Iraq).

On the night of 9–10 March 1945 a force of 334 B-29 bombers took off from the Mariana Islands and flew towards Tokyo. Three million dollars had been spent on the development and production of the B-29 – half as much again as on the atomic bomb. The military commanders wanted spectacular evidence of its potential, and the failed raids earlier in the year had increased the pressure on them. The planes had been stripped of their defensive capabilities: guns, gunners and ammunition were replaced by a double load of incendiaries. They flew in single file over Tokyo, and in two hours of continuous bombardment they created a firestorm worse than in Hamburg or Dresden. The bombs dropped what Robert Guillain, in *I Saw Tokyo Burning*, described as a 'flaming dew' that created 'a wash of dancing flames' across the roofs of the buildings. High winds helped the fires to spread until a firestorm was created. It took less than six hours to burn down sixteen square miles of the city. The American post-war Strategic Bombing Survey believed that 'more persons lost their lives by fire at Tokyo in a six-hour period than any time in the history of man'. In their summary, Tony Barrell and Rick Tanaka describe the effects of what the Japanese, more accurately, called 'slaughter bombing'. 'People, the fat in their skin bursting into flame, charring as they ran, dove

18. American B-29 bombers dropping huge quantities of bombs over Japan became an increasingly common sight in 1945.

into the Sumida river to drown rather than burn. Bridges sagged as the metal softened in the heat. Narrow canals boiled ... Some of the [bomber] crews in the final waves claimed they could smell burning flesh.' A quarter of the city was destroyed; ninety-seven thousand people were killed, a million injured, and a million and a half left homeless. Fire and 'petroleum gel', or napalm, had triumphed.

The bombing continued while the war in Europe ended. Japanese demoralisation was widespread. The Japanese air force stopped sending up fighters to resist the bombers. Between 8 and 9 million refugees fled from the towns to the country. It became so common to see USAAF planes crossing the sky that the Japanese people must have known the end was approaching, however it was envisaged. By mid-June most of the larger cities in Japan had been struck, though fatalities were sometimes much less than in Tokyo: 47 per cent of Yokohama, for example, was destroyed, but only five thousand civilians lost their lives. Forty per cent of all the 'urban structures' in Japan were burned, and some four hundred thousand civilians had been killed. In an unwitting repetition of the fears of the 1930s, *Time* magazine called the slaughter 'a dream come true'.

The Potsdam Declaration on 26 July spoke of 'prompt and utter destruction' if Japan did not surrender. Yet the bombing continued – until everything changed on the morning of 6 August. During the Spanish Civil War, bombing planes had been figured as cruciform bacilli, as gods, as birds of prey, and as vermin; George Barker had used the figure of 'Junker angels', and C. Day Lewis had written of bombers 'carry-ing harm in / Their wombs'. The pilots saw themselves differently; thus the plane carrying the first atomic bomb was named Enola Gay, after the pilot's mother. The bomb itself was called Little Boy and was designed, as in every little boy's dream, to do in one act of detonation what it had taken hundreds of planes and thousands of tonnes of high explosive to do at Hamburg, Tokyo and Dresden. The target was Hiroshima, where it exploded directly over the Shima Hospital. Forty-eight thousand buildings out of seventy-six thousand were completely destroyed. Most of the rest were severely damaged. A new scale of destruction challenged the power of words to describe it, as did that of the second atomic bomb, dropped on Nagasaki on 9 August.

GROUND ZERO

One Hiroshima survivor, unable to understand the sudden flattening of the city, 'thought it might have been ... the collapse of the earth which it was said would take place at the end of the world, and which I had read about as a child'. In fact it was the first act of the Cold War, a calculated demonstration of power directed at the Soviet Union, and one which in a different world might even have gratified the Japanese Emperor.

It was rapidly clear that it was not only the power of the atom bombs that made them different from previous weapons. Despite early attempts on the part of the United States authorities to deny and cover up the effects of radiation, and of the continued exposure of service personnel to it in the course of nuclear tests, the strange and fearful long-term consequences gradually become more widely known and more openly studied. But, as the Russians developed their own nuclear capability, the military and politicians on both sides in the Cold War were concerned more with maintaining and developing the destructive power of their

arsenals than with considering the likely effect of the manufacture and testing of their weapons, let alone their use on
civilians. And, as the power of successive generations of
atomic weapons increased, so the frontiers of people's safety
shrank. Whereas once, only a generation before, anywhere
within range of a bomber might be vulnerable, now there was
nowhere on the globe that would not experience the effects
of a nuclear war. When President Eisenhower was beginning what became known as his 'atoms for peace' campaign
in 1953, he rejected various drafts of speeches prepared for
him by C. D. Jackson, a specialist in psychological warfare,
saying, 'We don't want to scare the country to death.' But,
while they hid the programme behind talk of the 'enormous
benefits to mankind' which the atom would bring, scaring
some countries, at least – preferably to death – was exactly
what he wanted to do. It is what the threat of bombing does
best. And this time the threat of apocalypse seemed less of a
fantasy. The tradition of novels about the transformation of
civilisation into devastation through war was already well
established; nuclear weapons just made such a transformation seem more plausible and more urgent.

The genre is too vast for any attempt at a survey here;
novels such as Nevil Shute's *On the Beach*, and particularly
Stanley Kramer's film version, showed victims of a global
war condemned, like all life, to die in a matter of months. As
an imaginative issue in the 1950s, it was mostly confined to
science fiction, but the deep insecurities it provoked fed into
the psychology of the Cold War and informed the narrative
of countless horror films, comics and popular novels. Fear of
'the bomb' was replaced by fear of the Russians. Americans
believed that 'the nuclear bomb would be defeated by the
nuclear family'. Ostensibly, the bomb inaugurated a period

of prosperity and security in the USA. In 1946 the Manhattan Project was the subject of a docu-drama designed to show that Hiroshima had saved lives. Radiation and X-rays became confused in the realm of popular film and fiction, and there was a vague idea in the air that a new generation of medical discoveries was on its way. Only gradually did the idea of harmful mutation begin to find its way into the culture, via the *Incredible Hulk* and *The Incredible Shrinking Man*. In Britain, BBC television commissioned a feature-length film, *The War Game*, from Peter Watkins in 1966, then felt compelled to ban it – despite its winning an Academy Award – because it so powerfully succeeded in imagining and representing the likely nature and aftermath of a nuclear attack. The film used a pseudo-documentary framework, with interviews and with mock newsreels showing horrific episodes like policemen shooting injured survivors, and was described in the *Observer* as perhaps 'the most important film ever made'. It wasn't seen on the BBC for another twenty years, however. Nevertheless, the mere fact of the ban helped the cause of those opposed to nuclear weapons, and those who did manage to see the film did not easily forget it. Stanley Kubrick's film *Dr. Strangelove or: How I Learned to Stop Worrying and Love the Bomb*, a brilliant parody of the military approach to nuclear deterrence, was another response to what was increasingly seen, especially on the Left, as an irresponsible and potentially disastrous policy.

The difficulty of imagining a final disaster, nuclear extinction, and our part in it, remains a pressing one, however, and has continued to be a substantial element in literary and philosophical thinking over the last fifty years. From early imaginative attempts to weigh the moral issues involved in the new nuclear world, in novels like Aldous Huxley's *Ape*

19. *The last word in triumphalism: Slim Pickens, as B-52 Bomber pilot Major T. J. 'King' Kong, rides a hydrogen bomb in the closing sequence of the film* Dr. Strangelove or: How I Learned to Stop Worrying and Love the Bomb.

and Essence (1949) or William Golding's *Lord of the Flies* (1954) – whether to predict the re-emergence of some unchanging and fundamental bedrock of savagery, or to propagandise against the new world's politics – some recent writing has shifted towards thinking more bleakly about annihilation. Maurice Blanchot, Susan Sontag and Jacques Derrida have written productively about ways in which the mind can approach the unspeakable, and historians and psychoanalysts have made major contributions to what is an intractable problem. There seems to be no prospect of a let-up in the use of bombing, all over the world. The use of horrific quantities of napalm and chemical agents in Vietnam, in addition to various sophisticated anti-personnel and high-explosive bombs, merely extended the bombers' repertoire. Since then we have seen extensive use of bombers in the

Balkans, in Afghanistan, in Lebanon, in Iraq, and in other places around the world. Nothing in any of these places has improved the plight of the civilians – mostly poor, mostly innocent, all undeserving of the long-distance acts of power that deprive them of their children, parents, limbs, sight, homes, possessions, water, livelihoods: everything except an intense awareness of the injustice of being made into pawns in other people's political conflicts. That writers and film-makers, musicians and artists of all kinds are still drawn to the example of Guernica is a testimony to the way in which thinking about war and peace, present and future, still takes place under a sky that may one day fall on all our heads.

Epilogue

'A SCREAM THAT SHOULD
NEVER BE SILENCED'

In 1959 Martha Gellhorn wrote that

> despite official drivel about clean bombs and tactical
> nuclear weapons, anyone who can read a newspaper
> or listen to a radio knows that some of us mortals have
> the power to destroy the human race and man's home
> on earth ... How can anyone, anywhere, discount the
> irreversible folly of testing our nuclear bombs, or the
> promise of extinction if we use them in war? ... The
> world's leaders appear to have lost touch with life down
> here on the ground, to have forgotten the human beings
> they lead. Or perhaps the led – so numerous and so mute
> – have ceased to be quite real, not living people but cal-
> culated casualties.

In an attempt to do something, however symbolic, to
prevent the way of thinking that Gellhorn so eloquently
castigates, the town of Guernica has set up a foundation for
the study of peace. After his military victory in the civil war,
General Franco wanted absolutely nothing to do with for-
giveness or reconciliation. His crusade to reshape Spain was
founded on ruthless oppression. Instead of peace and recon-

ciliation, the defeated – those who weren't shot – would have to earn 'redemption'. As he wrote to the Italian ambassador, the authorities' first job would be the 'necessarily slow task of redemption and pacification, without which the military occupation will be largely useless. The moral redemption of the occupied zones will be long and difficult because in Spain the roots of anarchism are old and deep.' His vision was that the new regime he was imposing by such relentless force and ubiquitous cruelty would last for ever. He was the hand of God, agent of Spain's divine destiny. It took almost forty years for history to prove him wrong, and the wounds inflicted on Spain were deep. Spain in the 1940s and early 1950s was a place of mass executions, disease, starvation, slave labour. Memories of retribution are still fresh in some places – especially in the Basque country, which has still not achieved the independence it was seeking in the 1930s.

But Guernica has stimulated some of the many positive contributions of the last three decades. The Comisión Gernika was established in 1979 with the hope of obtaining some gesture of reconciliation or apology from the Bundestag, the German parliament. It took time, but in 1987 the leader of Germany's Green Party, Petra Kelly, with Gert Bastian, introduced a motion calling for acknowledgement of the bombing and for some tangible form of reconciliation. That same year, fifty years after the bombing, the Basque parliament agreed to finance the Gernika Gogoratuz peace research centre. Guernica was declared a city of peace and was twinned with the south-west-German city of Pforzheim, site of one of the most devastating Allied bombing attacks in the Second World War, on the evening of 23 February 1945, when half a million high-explosive and incendiary bombs were dropped, creating a firestorm in which about seventeen thousand people (20 per cent of the town's population) were killed and 83 per cent of the buildings destroyed. (The British Bombing Survey estimated that the proportion of buildings destroyed was 'probably the greatest ... in one raid during the war'.) The following year Petra Kelly led a Green Party initiative, supported by the German Social Democrats, to reach a consensus with the other parties in the Bundestag for a proposal for a gesture of peace and friendship from the Federal Republic of Germany to Guernica. The proposal was discussed three times in the parliament, but in the end it was an alternative, watered-down, motion from the Christian Democrats which prevailed and was adopted. Although there was a certain amount of foot-dragging at the national level, the local initiative between Guernica and Pforzheim has flourished, as has the Gernika Gogoratuz. Guernica has also been twinned with Wustorf, the original base of the Condor Legion. Then, in November 1996, eight years after the first resolution, the Bundestag revised its decision, recognised German responsibility for the bombing, and voted 3 million marks towards a sports centre in Guernica.

GERMANY APOLOGISES

Finally, in a dramatic gesture on 27 April 1997, Roman Herzog, president of the Federal Republic of Germany, stood in the Plaza del Mercado in the centre of Guernica, where the first bombs had fallen sixty years before, and for the first time publicly acknowledged his country's responsibility for the bombing of the town in 1937. Present were some of the survivors of the bombing, as various newspapers reported the next day. 'We thought we would die, and began to pray together, but we couldn't hear our voices above the bombs,' remembered one. 'The planes came very low,' remembered Itziar de Arzanegi, who was eleven years old in 1937. 'We could even see the goggles on the pilot's faces. One old woman didn't run, and instead screamed curses at them. She was hit by bullets.' The mayor of Guernica, Eduardo Vallejo, who was only a baby at the time of the raid, explained that the people of Guernica 'want the world to remember so it does not happen again. It is a scream that should never be silenced.'

Picasso forbade the display of his painting in Spain until the country once again had 'public liberties and democratic institutions'. It was moved from New York to Madrid on 25 October 1981, on the centenary of Picasso's birth. In 1985 the estate of Nelson A. Rockefeller presented the United Nations headquarters in New York with a tapestry reproduction of *Guernica*, which was hung outside the Security Council chamber. As the Security Council was gathering on 5 February 2003 to listen to the US Secretary of State, Colin Powell, present the American case for the war against Iraq, workers covered the tapestry with a blue cloth and the flags of member nations. UN diplomats said that pressure had been brought to bear by the United States, after administration officials realised that the picture had been shown on television round the world as a backdrop to chief weapons inspector Hans Blix's presentation a week earlier. US spokesmen denied this.

FURTHER READING

INTRODUCTION

The epigraph comes from Martha Gellhorn's eloquent introduction to a collection of her war journalism, written between
1936 and 1945, *The Face of War* (London, 1959). Everybody
ought to read it. Fernando Arrabal's play (originally written
in the 1950s and published in French in 1961), translated by
Barbara Wright, was published in his *Plays Volume 2* (London,
1967). Bertrand Russell quotes Giacomo Leopardi's poem 'La
Ginestra' in a translation by R. C. Trevelyan, who subsequently
published a collection of Leopardi's verse in English. Russell's
Power: A New Social Analysis (London, 1938) is still worth
reading. The best historical introduction to the 1930s is Piers
Brendon, *The Dark Valley: A Panorama of the 1930s* (London,
2000); it also contains well-delineated outline accounts of the
Abyssinian conflict and the Spanish Civil War. For a broader
view, there is John Stevenson, *British Society, 1914–1945*
(London, 1984). A contemporary account of the decade that
makes quite lively reading is Malcolm Muggeridge's *The
Thirties: Britain 1930–1940* (London, 1940). The much-quoted
phrase by W. H. Auden is to be found in his poem 'September
1, 1939', first published in *Another Time* (London, 1940). Louis
MacNeice's *Autumn Journal* (London, 1939) offers a witty and
engaged verse reflection of the last years of the decade.

One of the best introductory accounts of the Spanish Civil War itself is Antony Beevor, *The Battle for Spain: The Spanish Civil War 1936–1939* (London, 2006). Paul Preston, who has written brilliantly and extensively on the civil war, provides a lucid and detailed explanation of the events leading up to it in *The Coming of the Spanish Civil War: Reform, Reaction and Revolution in the Second Republic* (2nd edn, London, 1994). Leah Manning's report was published by Victor Gollancz in 1935, under the title *What I Saw in Spain*. Burnett Bolloten is quoted from *The Spanish Revolution: The Left and the Struggle for Power during the Civil War* (Chapel Hill, NC, 1979). The contributors to the pamphlet *Spain and Us* included J. B. Priestley, Rebecca West, Stephen Spender, Ethel Mannin and T. F. Powys. Heinrich Mann's comments were published in Paris in the literary magazine *Mot* (Paris, 1939). Muriel Rukeyser's *Mediterranean* was first published in *New Masses* (1938), and reprinted the same year as a pamphlet in support of the Medical Bureau to aid Spanish Democracy, which was building American hospitals in Spain.

CHAPTER 1: 'GUERNICA'S THERMITE RAIN'

The number of books and articles written about Guernica and the Spanish Civil War is huge. Apart from the books mentioned above, the most helpful guidance is provided by one of the foundational works, Hugh Thomas's masterly *The Spanish Civil War* (London, 1961). Paul Preston's biography *Franco* (London, 1993) provides a brilliant account of the man behind it all. The two outstanding books about Guernica are G. L. Steer's *The Tree of Gernika: A Field Study of Modern War* (London, 1938) and Herbert H. Southworth, *Guernica! Guernica! A Study of Journalism, Diplomacy, Propaganda, and History* (Berkeley and London, 1977). These are both essential reading for any study of this topic, and both have accordingly been much quarried by later writers, including me. There's also a very good biography of Steer by Nicholas Rankin, *Telegram from Guernica: The Extraordinary Life of George Steer, War Correspondent* (London, 2003). For further detail of the bombing, see Vicente Talón, *El holocausto de Guernica* (Barcelona, 1987). There is a selection of basic documents, and an extraordinary collection of photographs, in *Gernika 1937, sustrai erreak* (Guernica, 1987). The best guide to the intricacies of Spain's internal divisions is Helen Graham, *The Spanish Republic at War 1936–1939* (Cambridge, 2002); Tom Buchanan, *Britain and the Spanish Civil War* (Cambridge, 1997) provides a good account of the differing responses to the war in Britain and also has an excellent annotated bibliography. Hansard provides the full record of debates in both Houses of Parliament.

First-hand and oral accounts bring events to life in Ronald Fraser's *Blood of Spain: The Experience of Civil War, 1936–1939* (London, 1979) and in Jesus Cava Mesa, *Memoria colectiva del bombardeo de Gernika* (Guernica, 1996). Gordon Thomas and Max Morgan-Witts used oral evidence for their rather sensationalised, semi-fictional recreation of *The Day Guernica Died* (London, 1975); some of their claims are attacked by Castor Uriarte Aguirreamalloa in *Bombas y mentiras sobre Guernica* (Bilbao, 1976). Alberto de Onaindia's memories are in the first volume of his *Capitulos de mi vida, hombre de paz en la guerra* (Buenos Aires, 1973). The two recent books on Picasso's painting are Gijs van Hensbergen's *Guernica: The Biography of a Twentieth-Century Icon* (London, 2004) and *Picasso's War* by Russell Martin (New York, 2002). There is a good article on the ways in which Guernica's symbolic importance developed, 'Guernica como simbolo' by Alberto Reig, in Carmelo Garitaonandia and Jose Luis de la Granja (eds.), *La Guerra Civil en el Pais Vasco: 50 años después* (Bilbao, 1987), a book which also contains other helpful contributions. To supplement what Steer has to say about the history of the Basque country, it's useful to read Mark Kurlansky's lively account in *A Basque History of the World* (London, 1999), and Juan Pablo Fusi's chapter on 'The Basque Question' in *Revolution and the Civil War in Spain 1931–1939*, ed. Paul Preston (London, 1984). Noel Monks's memoir is *Eye Witness* (Muller, 1955), and Virginia Cowles described her encounter with the outspoken Nationalist officer in *Looking for Trouble* (London, 1941). The case for the denial of the bombing is set out in *Guernica: Official Report of the Commission Appointed by the National Government*, Introduction by Sir Arnold Lunn (London, 1938), which also has a number of photographs which speak for themselves.

The Spanish campaign against Abd el-Krim is well described in James S. Corum and Wray R. Johnson, *Airpower in Small Wars: Fighting Insurgents and Terrorists* (Lawrence, Kan., 2003). Jesús Salas Larrazàbal, *Air War over Spain* (London, 1974) provides a good introduction to the role of airpower in the civil war. James S. Corum's article on 'The Spanish Civil War: Lessons Learned and Not Learned by the Great Powers', in *Journal of Military History*, 62 (April 1998), pp. 313–34, is a neat summary of the war's military usefulness to those taking part illegally or observing from a distance. Much of the material on the Condor Legion is derived from Corum's book, *The Luftwaffe: Creating the Operational Air War 1918–1940* (Lawrence, Kan., 1997), especially Chapter 6. The other good account is by Raymond Proctor, *Hitler's Luftwaffe in the Spanish Civil War* (New York, 1983), especially

Chapter 9. Klaus Maier, *Guernica 26.4.1937: Die deutsche Intervention in Spanien und der 'Fall Guernica'* (Freiburg, 1975) provides what is still the fullest German account. There is a great deal of technical information, not all of it reliable, in Karl Ries and Hans Ring, *The Legion Condor: A History of the Luftwaffe in the Spanish Civil War* (West Chester, Pa., 1992), but only if you can put up with its relentlessly disparaging attitude towards the Republicans. Gerald Howson's *Arms for Spain: The Untold Story of the Spanish Civil War* (London, 1998) has a useful chapter on 'air-mindedness' in Spain. Robert Whealey's *Hitler and Spain: The Nazi Role in the Spanish Civil War 1936–1939* (Lexington, Ky., 1989) includes a good summary of the Legion's role in Spain. Hubert Brieden, Heidi Dettinger and Marion Hirschfeld bring the story up to date in *'Ein voller Erfolg der Luftwaffe': Die Vernichtung Guernicas und deutsche Traditionspflege* (Neustadt, 1997). The original German history of the Legion, Werner Beumelburg's *Kampf um Spanien*, was published in 1939 to celebrate the airmen's triumphant return to Berlin and contains some interesting material. It claims that the Republicans fired the town after the Germans had bombed it.

On non-intervention, see Douglas Little, *Malevolent Neutrality: The United States, Great Britain, and the Outbreak of the Spanish Civil War* (Ithaca, NY, 1985) and subsequent work by Enrique Moradiellos, such as his essay on the British perception of Franco, in Paul Preston and A. Mackenzie (eds.), *The Republic Besieged: Civil War in Spain, 1936–1939* (Edinburgh, 1991). A good place to find out more about the Catholic Church's support for Franco is Herbert Southworth's *Conspiracy and the Spanish Civil War* (London, 2002), in which the author reveals an 'interlocking system of Catholic propaganda exchanges in Western Europe and

North America'. (Eyre & Spottiswoode, the London publishers who published most of the pro-Franco propaganda during the civil war, had their offices and archives destroyed by bombs during the Blitz.)

George Orwell's impressions of Barcelona come from *Homage to Catalonia* (London, 1938). Franz Borkenau's *The Spanish Cockpit: An Eye-Witness Account of the Social and Political Conflicts of the Spanish Civil War*, still one of the best books to read on the subject, appeared in London in 1937. The treatment of the civil war in British newsreels is the subject of Anthony Aldgate's *Cinema and History: British Newsreels and the Spanish Civil War* (London, 1979). The two Basque poems, 'Gernika' by Telesforo Monzon and Mikel Zarate's '1937, Apirilak 26', are both printed in S. Onaindia, *Gernika* (Bilbao, 1987). The versions here are based on literal translations kindly provided by Pablo Perez d'Ors.

Some of the poetry inspired by the destruction of Guernica is reprinted in Valentine Cunningham, *The Penguin Book of Spanish Civil War Verse* (Harmondsworth, 1980). For an earlier harvest, see *Poems for Spain*, ed. John Lehmann and Stephen Spender (London, 1939). Barry Stavis's play *Refuge* was published in a mimeographed edition by the Left Book Club Theatre Guild in 1938. MacLeish's *Air Raid* was published in New York the same year, and in London a year later. Hermann Kesten's novel could not, of course, be published in Germany. It was first published in Holland, as *Die Kinder von Guernica*, in 1938; Geoffrey Dunlop's translation came out in London in 1939. Sarah Campion (the pseudonym of Mary Coulton) wrote a number of very interesting novels in the 1930s and '40s, including *Thirty Million Gas Masks* (London, 1937).

CHAPTER 2: CIVILISATION AND ITS DISCONTENTS

Stanley Baldwin's speech is transcribed from Hansard, 10 November 1932. Along with *The Times* digital archive, Hansard is an invaluable record. Frank Morison's *War on Great Cities: A Study of the Facts* (London, 1937) is a sober assessment of the bombing of London during the First World War. F. S. Flint's poem was included in his collection *Otherworld* (London, 1920), and Laurence Binyon's poem can be found in full in *The Four Years* (London, 1919). *Zeppelin Nights* by Violet Hunt and Ford Madox Hueffer (later Ford Madox Ford) was published in London in 1916, and deserves to be reprinted. Proust's description of the Zeppelin raid is taken from the final volume of the new Penguin Proust, *Finding Time Again*, translated by Ian Patterson (London, 2003). Sidney Rogerson's *Propaganda in the Next War* was published in London in 1938. Many of the central texts – writings and speeches – in the history of air warfare (or extracts from them) are usefully gathered together in the 900-page anthology edited by Eugene M. Emme, *The Impact of Air Power* (Princeton, 1959). There is a good overview of all the historical material in Philip S. Meilinger, 'The Historiography of Airpower: Theory and Doctrine', in *Journal of Military History* 64 (April 2000), pp. 467–502. For an extremely well-informed and wide-ranging view of the whole history, the best book to read is Tami Davis Biddle's *Rhetoric and Reality in Air Warfare* (Princeton, 2002). The best account of the most important theorists is in Azar Gat, *Fascist and Liberal Versions of War* (Oxford, 1998); on RAF policy between wars, see also Robin Higham, *The Military Intellectuals*, especially Chapter 6. Churchill's writings can be found in the Eugene Emme anthology, and in Sir Winston Churchill, *Collected Essays*, ed. Michael Wolff (London, 1976), vol. 1: *Churchill and War*. The

English translation of Giulio Douhet's *Il Dominio dell'Aria*, *Command of the Air* by Dino Ferrari (New York, 1942; London, 1943) includes the additional pieces Douhet wrote after its first publication in 1921. Other important contributions to the debate include J. F. C. Fuller, *The Reformation of War* (London, 1923), Basil Liddell Hart, *Paris; or the Future of War* (London, 1925); P. R. C. Groves, *Behind the Smoke Screen* (London, 1934) and three of J. M. Spaight's books, *Air Power and the Cities* (London, 1930), *Air Power in the Next War* (London, 1938) and *Air Power Can Disarm* (London, 1948). Robert Donington and Barbara Donington, *The Citizen Faces War* (London, 1936) is one of the first practical assessments of civil defence.

James S. Corum and Wray R. Johnson's *Airpower in Small Wars: Fighting Insurgents and Terrorists* (Lawrence, Kan., 2003) is a good introduction to the use of air power in colonies, and David Omissi's *Air Power and Colonial Control: The Royal Air Force 1919–1939* (Manchester, 1990) provides a wealth of gruesome detail. Charles Townshend provides a closer focus on 'frightfulness' in his essay 'Civilisation and "Frightfulness": Air Control in the Middle East Between the Wars', in Chris Wrigley (ed.), *Essays in Honour of A. J. P. Taylor* (London, 1986). Orwell's comments on euphemism are extracted from his essay 'Politics and the English Language', first published in *Horizon* in April 1946. For the implications of air warfare for British domestic and foreign policy, see Uri Bialer, *The Shadow of the Bomber: The Fear of Air Attack and British Politics 1932–1939* (London, 1980), and for an excellent historical contextualisation of the place of air-mindedness in British culture see David Edgerton, *England and the Aeroplane: An Essay on a Militant and Technological Nation* (Basingstoke, 1991). Peter Fritzche provides a similarly impressive survey for Germany in *A Nation of Fliers: German Aviation and the*

Popular Imagination (Cambridge, Mass., 1992); Chapter 5 is particularly useful. Le Corbusier's *Aircraft* (London, 1935) shows very clearly how a bird's-eye view can remove one from social reality. The cultural impact of air warfare can be followed up in more detail in Michael Paris, *From the Wright Brothers to Top Gun: Aviation, Nationalism and Popular Cinema* (Manchester, 1995), Robert Wohl, *A Passion for Wings: Aviation and the Western Imagination, 1908–1918* (New Haven, 1994) and Laurence Goldstein, *The Flying Machine and Modern Literature* (Basingstoke, 1986). Tom Wintringham translated and introduced F. O. Mitschke's *Blitzkrieg* (London, 1941), which is the founding document of the Condor Legion's tactics. There is lots of useful and wide-ranging material in Joanna Bourke, *Fear: A Cultural History* (London, 2005), and I have drawn freely on Leo Bersani's Introduction to Freud's *Civilisation and its Discontents* (London, 2002).

Two outstanding works laid the foundations for all subsequent study of air-war fiction in the interwar years. The first is I. F. Clarke, *Voices Prophesying War 1763–1984* (1966; 2nd edn, Oxford, 1992), and the second is the short essay by Martin Ceadel, 'Popular Fiction and the Next War, 1918–1939', in Frank Glover Smith (ed.), *Class, Culture and Social Change* (Brighton, 1980). C. J. Simer's unpublished 1999 PhD thesis from the University of Minnesota, 'Apocalyptic Visions: Fear of Aerial Attack in Britain 1920–1938', provides a lot more detail, and adds a few more titles. I am much indebted to all three writers. Sven Lindqvist's *A History of Bombing* (London, 2001) is an admirable (if schematic) history in strangely user-friendly form. Charles Madge's poem 'Loss', first published in 1934, is reprinted in Madge's *Of Love, Time and Places: Selected Poems* (London, 1994); Stephen Spender's 'From All These Events' is in *Poems* (London, 1933), and Rex

Warner's poem was the first in his *Poems and Contradictions* (London, 1945). H. B. Mallalieu's poem was printed in *Poems for Spain*, ed. John Lehmann and Stephen Spender (London, 1939). Adrian Stokes's *Colour and Form* came out in 1937, the year before Upward's *Journey to the Border*.

The use of bombs and chemical weapons in Abyssinia is documented in G. L. Steer (again), *Caesar in Abyssinia* (London, 1936), and in Thomas M. Coffey, *Lion by the Tail: The Story of the Italian–Ethiopian War* (London, 1974). Vittorio Mussolini's exploits are recorded in his *Voli sulle ambe* (Florence, 1937); I used the German translation, *Bomber über Abessinien* (Munich, 1937). (I don't know where Russell found the famous comments by Bruno Mussolini he cites.) Two reports by Shuhsi Hsü, *The War Conduct of the Japanese* (Hankow, 1938) and *Three Weeks of Cantonese Bombings* (Shanghai, Hong Kong and Singapore, 1939) provided details about events in China, as did Robert B. Ekvall's powerful report 'The Bombing of Chungking', in *Asia*, 39, 8 (August 1939), pp. 471–3. W. H. Auden and Christopher Isherwood's *Journey to a War* (London, 1939) contains photos as well as poems and the narrative of their time in China.

CHAPTER 3: WAR BEGINS AT HOME

The chapter title is stolen from Mass-Observation, from Charles Madge and Tom Harrisson, *War Begins at Home* (London, 1940), which is a wonderful record of what people were thinking during the first year of the war. (Between 1937 and the late 1940s, Mass-Observation – it was usually, but not always, hyphenated – used volunteer observers to carry out a series of investigations into all aspects of people's lives, including studies of the pub, work, jokes, attitudes, and all sorts of leisure activities, some of which were published in book form, or as reports. There is a rich and extensive archive of volunteers' responses and diaries at the University of Sussex.) Wesley K. Wark is good on appeasement in *The Ultimate Enemy: British Intelligence and Nazi Germany, 1933–1939* (Ithaca, NY, 1985). Roosevelt's radio speech can be found in Eugene M. Emme's anthology *The Impact of Air Power* (Princeton, 1959). For the allied bombing campaign, see Sir Robert Saundby, *Air Bombardment: The Story of its Development* (London, 1961); a more up-to-date and nuanced account is John Pimlott's essay on 'The Theory and Practice of Strategic Bombing', in Colin McInnes and G. D. Sheffield (eds.), *Warfare in the Twentieth Century: Theory and Practice* (London, 1988). A fuller statement of the moral arguments will be found in Stephen A. Garrett, *Ethics and Airpower in World War II: The British Bombing of German Cities* (Basingstoke, 1993); A. C. Grayling surveys recent work on the question in his excellent *Among the Dead Cities: Was the Allied Bombing of Civilians in WWII a Necessity or a Crime?* (London, 2006). W. G. Sebald surveys various German attempts to put experience into words in *On the Natural History of Destruction*, trans. Anthea Bell (London, 2003). Vera Brittain's account of the early part of the Blitz is in *England's Hour* (London, 1941); her polemic against bombing, *Seed of Chaos: What Mass Bombing Really Means* (London, 1944), has been republished in Vera Brittain, *One Voice* (London and New York, 2005). For a good sense of life under bombardment in Britain, see Tom Harrisson, *Living Through the Blitz* (London, 1976), Constantine FitzGibbon, *London's Burning* (London, 1970) and Philip Ziegler, *London at War, 1939–1945* (London, 1995). Angus Calder's *The People's War* (London, 1969) is still worth reading, as is his more recent *The Myth of the Blitz* (London, 1991). The best account of cultural life during the war is still Robert Hewison's *Under Siege: Literary Life in London 1939–1945* (London, 1977). Mollie Panter-Downes, *London War Notes 1939–1945*, ed. William Shawn (London, 1973), give us a vivid picture of daily life.

For the bombing of Japan, some good books to read, out of the hundreds that have been written, are Robert Guillain, *I Saw Tokyo Burning: An Eyewitness Narrative from Pearl Harbor to Hiroshima*, trans. William Byron (London, 1981); the article by Thomas R. Searle, '"It Made a Lot of Sense to Kill Skilled Workers": The Firebombing of Tokyo in March 1945', in *Journal of Military History*, 66 (January 2002), pp. 103–34; Robert Jungk, *Brighter Than a Thousand Suns* (London, 1958); Wilfred Burchett, *Shadows of Hiroshima* (London, 1983) and Tony Barrell and Rick Tanaka, *Higher than Heaven: Japan, War and Everything* (Strawberry Hills, NSW, 1995). Lewis Mumford's *Programme for Survival* (New York, 1946) was one of the first meditations on the implications of the atomic bomb.

EPILOGUE: 'A SCREAM THAT SHOULD NEVER BE SILENCED'

The history of the reconciliation between Germany and Guernica is set out in Michael Kasper, *Gernika y Alemania: Historia de una reconciliación* (Gernika, 1998) and in Gert Bastian and Petra Kelly (eds.), *Guernica und die Deutschen* (Hamburg, 1992). For information about the work of the peace centre in Guernica, and about its publications, see its website at http://www.gernikagogoratuz.org.

All translations are by the author, unless otherwise indicated.

LIST OF ILLUSTRATIONS

While every effort has been made to contact copyright-holders of illustrations, the author and publishers would be grateful for information about any illustrations where they have been unable to trace them, and would be glad to make amendments in further editions.

ACKNOWLEDGEMENTS

Thanks to Mary Beard, Peter Carson, Alison Carter, Andrew Crozier, Jenny Diski, David Edgerton, Natasha Fairweather, Stephen Legg, Julia Lovell, Rod Mengham, Pablo Perez d'Ors, Susan Pennybacker, Lyndsey Stonebridge, Deborah Thom and Clair Wills.

INDEX

PROFILES IN HISTORY

The *Profiles in History* series will explore iconic events
and relationships in history. Each book will start from
the historical moment: what happened? But each will
focus too on the fascinating and often surprising
afterlife of the story concerned.

Profiles in History is under the general editorship of Mary Beard.

Already available:
David Horspool: *King Alfred: Burnt Cakes and Other Legends*
James Sharpe: *Remember, Remember: A Cultural History of
Guy Fawkes Day*

Forthcoming:
Claire Pettitt: *Dr. Livingstone, I Presume? Missionaries,
Journalists, Explorers, and Empire*
Greg Woolf: *Et Tu, Brute? A Short History of Political Murder*
Christopher Prendergast, *The Fourteenth of July*